Dodie Roe

Eat
to
live

Longman

First published 1983
Third impression 1986, with amendments
ISBN 0 582 22177 3

Set in 10/12 pt Linotron 202 Helvetica Roman

Produced by Longman Singapore Publishers (Pte) Ltd.
Printed in Singapore

Acknowledgements

We are grateful to The Society of Authors as the representative of the
Literary Trustees of Walter de la Mare for permission to use an extract
from the poem 'Miss T' on page 104.

Illustrated by Dennis Reader

Contents

How to use this book

You will find these signs in this book to show you what to do:

Work to do in your own books or folders. Always put a heading for your work and write neatly and fully so that you can look back and understand it later.

Experiments or investigation to carry out. You will probably need to record what you do and the results in your own book or folder.

Key facts to remember. These are the important food facts that you should try to learn and remember.

1 Why do we need food?

Do you know that in Britain we eat more sweets per person than in any other country?

Do you know that nearly all British children have some tooth decay and that 25 per cent of today's five-year-olds will probably need false teeth before they are twenty?

Do you know that the average person eats 180 g butter, 90 g margarine and three loaves a week?

Do you know that we eat 50 kg of sugar a year and that about half this amount is used in the home, and half is used in making cakes, sweets and ice cream?

Do you know how many people in this country are over-weight?

Do you know why people become overweight?

Do you know that two-thirds of the world's population do not get enough to eat?

If the answer to any of these questions is 'no' then you need to know more about **nutrition**.

Nutrition means knowing about what foods to eat, and how the body uses food.

How do **you** choose food?

Think about the type of food you have at lunchtime on an ordinary school day.

Write down this list and tick your answer:

Do you have
- a school lunch (describe what you eat)
- something from the school tuck shop
- fish and chips
- chips on their own
- a packed lunch of meat, salad, fruit
- a packed lunch of sandwiches or rolls
- some other sort of packed lunch
- something on toast
- some other type of lunch (say what)

Do you have this because it is
- cheap
- quick
- slimming
- prepared for you
- all your friends have the same
- you just like it

How much would you expect your lunch to cost?

Many things make us choose food — time, money, convenience, taste, but the most important one of all should be **nutrition.** We should eat a **variety** of foods so that we have a little of each of the **nutrients** the body needs in order to survive.

What do we mean by nutrients?

Let's think about a cake.

This cake is made from a **recipe.**

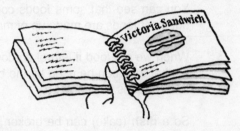

The recipe tells us what we need to make the cake and how to do it.

If we studied the recipe we would know which foods or **ingredients** are used to make the cake. The ingredients for a Victoria sandwich would be

eggs
sugar
flour
fat

Each ingredient is made up of **nutrients**. We cannot see them, but we can carry out tests to show they are there. You will see some of these tests later in the book.

The nutrients in eggs are called

protein	**vitamin A**
fat	**vitamin B1**
iron	**vitamin B2**
	vitamin D

The nutrients in sugar are called
    carbohydrate

The nutrients in flour are called
> **protein**
> **carbohydrate**
> **fat**
> **calcium**
> **iron**
> **vitamin B1**

You can see that some foods contain only one nutrient, but most foods are made up of many different nutrients.

When we eat food it is broken down into these nutrients, so that they can be used by the body. We shall see how this happens in Chapter 9.

So a **dish** (cake) can be broken down into **ingredients** which can be broken down into **nutrients**.

 This table shows the most important nutrients that the body needs, and some of the foods which provide them.

The body needs nutrients for	These are called	They are found in
Building and repair of the body	**Protein**	Meat, fish, cheese, milk, eggs, peas, beans, lentils, soya, nuts, bread
	Minerals	
Building teeth and bones	(i) calcium	Milk, cheese, flour, cabbage, eggs, fish bones
Building blood	(ii) iron	Liver, corned beef, meat, baked beans, curry powder, dried fruits, chocolate, black treacle, eggs, cabbage, oily fish

Energy	**Carbohydrate** (i) starch	Flour, rice, pasta, potatoes, cereals,
	(ii) sugar (not needed in the body, but often eaten in)	sugar, jam, syrup, sweets, chocolate, tinned foods
	Fats	Butter, lard, margarine, oil, oily fish, milk, cheese, fat on meat, chocolate

Health and protection	**Vitamins**	
For healthy sight, skin, helping to stop infection, healing of wounds	**A**	Margarine, herrings, milk, carrots, apricots, prunes, tomatoes, butter
For healthy nerves, skin and muscle. To help the body use foods which provide energy	**B1**	Bread, yeast, marmite, meat, eggs, milk, green vegetables
For growth, health of eyes and mouth	**B2**	Marmite, green vegetables, milk, eggs, beer, peanuts
For healthy gums and skin and to help stop infection and heal wounds	**C**	Fruit, especially oranges, lemons, grapefruit, blackcurrants, green vegetables, potatoes, tomatoes, green peppers
For building strong bones	**D**	Margarine, butter, oily fish, eggs, cheese, sunlight
Replacing the salt lost in perspiration	**Minerals** sodium chloride (salt)	Table salt, salty foods

The body also needs **fibre** and **water.**

These are not nutrients but are very important for the body.

Fibre makes us feel full, speeds up the passage of foods through the body and helps prevent bowel diseases, gall stones, gastric ulcers and coronary heart disease.

Water About 70 per cent of the body's weight is water. Water is lost in perspiration and must be replaced by the body. At least 1 litre of liquid should be drunk daily. This can be as tea, coffee, squash or other drinks as well as just water. We can last several weeks without food, but we would last only a few days without water.

Will any one food provide all these nutrients?

No. This is why we cannot live on chips or ice cream or whatever is our favourite food. The food which comes nearest to providing them all is milk. Look at the table and see how many times milk appears. But even milk does not provide all the nutrients, as you can see, so as we get older more foods have to be introduced into the diet. Besides, a diet of just milk would soon get boring. So we need a variety of foods in order to make sure we get some of all the nutrients and have a **healthy diet.** Diet isn't anything to do with slimming. It just means the food we eat.

What do we mean by variety?

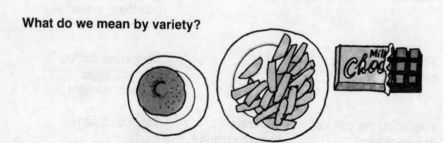

Do you think this shows variety?

These are different foods – **but** – they would not make a very healthy diet.

For a healthy diet eat foods from each of these groups

milk
cheese
yoghurt

meat
fish
eggs
beans
lentils
nuts

fresh or frozen fruit
 and vegetables
salad foods

wholemeal bread
cereals
spaghetti (wholemeal)
rice
potatoes

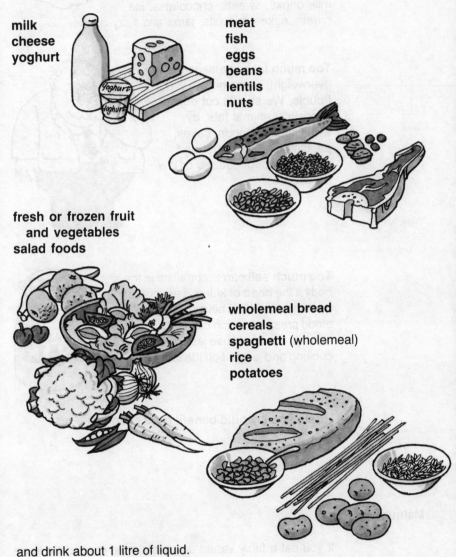

and drink about 1 litre of liquid.

Too much of some foods can be as bad as not eating the right food.

Too much sugar can harm teeth
and lead to weight problems,
heart trouble and diabetes. We
can eat less by cutting down on
sugar in tea or coffee and other
milk drinks, sweets, chocolates, ice
cream, cakes, biscuits, jams and fizzy drinks.

Too much fat can make us
overweight, cause heart
trouble. We should cut down
especially animal fats, by
avoiding fried foods, cakes,
pastries, cream, butter and
cheese (except cottage or low
fat cheese).

Too much salt can accumulate in the
body if the heart or kidneys are not
working properly. This may cause high
blood pressure which can lead to heart
attacks. We could use less salt in
cooking and leave it off the table.

Most people would benefit from eating 10% less
    sugar
    fat
    salt

Malnutrition

If you eat a fairly varied diet it is almost impossible to be
short of protein, vitamins or minerals in this country. It is
more likely that you are eating too many foods containing
fat and sugar.

Finicky feeders or crash dieters should beware – they are the ones who are likely to be missing out on important nutrients and this could damage their health.

In countries where a variety of foods is not available a lack of all nutrients can lead to a disease called **marasmus**. We call this a deficiency disease. It is caused by malnutrition because the diet doesn't contain (is deficient in) nutrients. Malnutrition can be caused by too few **or** too many nutrients.

In the chapters which follow you will be learning more about **eating to live**.

See how you're doing so far . . .

1 Look back at the lunch you chose on page 6. After what you have learned so far do you think the meal you chose shows variety?

Try scoring your meal as follows. Some foods may score more than once. For example potatoes would score 2 points for carbohydrate and 3 points for vitamin C.

For each food containing
        protein, score 5
        calcium, score 4
        iron, score 4
        fibre, score 4
        vitamin A, score 3
        vitamin B, score 3
        vitamin C, score 3
        vitamin D, score 3
        carbohydrate (starch), score 2
        fats, score 1
        water, score 1
        sugar, score 0

If you scored:
30 or more, and most of your score came from protein, calcium, iron, vitamins and fibre then this is excellent. The meal has provided a variety of nutrients — keep it up.

25–30 Very good. Try to push up the high scoring foods.
20–25 Take another look at your meal and see how you could include more of the high scoring foods.
15–25 You must have eaten either very little or only low scoring foods, so now think about the foods you could add to provide more variety.
Under 15 Read this chapter again!

2 Write these headings in your book:
   Nutrient
   Food/ingredient
   Dish
   Recipe

Put these under the correct heading:
   potatoes
   calcium
   50g flour, 50g sugar, 50g margarine, 1 egg
   protein
   vitamin B1
   toast
   spaghetti bolognese
   carbohydrate
   rice
   yoghurt

2 Does it matter what we eat?

You may not be responsible for planning and choosing meals now, but at some time you will probably be choosing food not only for yourself, but also for others.

To make sure you have a sensible diet you will need to know about
choosing food
buying food
making food into meals

Choosing food

In the last chapter we looked at some of our reasons for choosing food.

Write down those you can remember.

Here are some other reasons why you might choose particular sorts of food.

foreign travel

where you live

family habits or traditions

'old wives' tales

equipment available for cooking

lifestyle

food supply

religion

television and advertising

Find out

1 Find out which religions have special food laws and why they have them, e.g. why Jews do not eat pork.

2 Make a list of kitchen equipment which might affect the sort of meals you eat, e.g. a pressure cooker.

3 Compare an average day's food that you eat with that of someone in India.

4 Make a list of 'old wives' tales' about food that you, your friends and family know, e.g. 'Crusts make your hair curl'.

5 Find out the names of some traditional dishes and how they started, e.g. Yorkshire pudding.

6 Watch some advertisements for food on television. Can you guess whom they are aimed at?

7 Many foreign dishes have become part of our diet. Make a list of those you know and the countries they come from, e.g. curry from India. See if you can work out why these dishes are eaten in each country.

Buying food

When we go out to buy food we have the choice of buying **fresh food** or **convenience foods. Fresh foods** are those that have come to us straight from the land or sea. **Convenience foods** are foods that have been processed and packaged in such a way that they save time and effort.

Take potatoes for example. We could buy fresh potatoes or we could buy
> a tin of potatoes or
> a packet of dehydrated (dried) potatoes or
> frozen chips or
> frozen croquettes or
> frozen oven-cook chips.

The **tinned**, **dried** and **frozen** potatoes are all examples of convenience foods. Other convenience foods are **AFD** (**accelerated freeze dried** — a combination of freezing and drying) and **packet mixes** (e.g. a cake mix in which all or most of the ingredients are in the packet).

Write down the convenience food forms in which the following may be bought. e.g. **peas** – frozen, canned, dried

> **steak and kidney pies**
> **potatoes**
> **chocolate cake**
> **carrots**
> **steamed pudding**
> **custard**
> **beef curry**
> **rice pudding**
> **apple sauce**
> **apricots**

Are convenience foods as nutritious as fresh foods?

If you buy fresh foods you know that you should get all the nutrients supplied by that food.

This is not always true with convenience foods – for example processed peas contain less vitamin C than fresh peas because they are dried before they are canned, and vitamin C is destroyed during drying.

Some foods have the nutrients that are lost during processing added back to them. For example synthetic (man-made) vitamin C is often added to dried potato to replace that which is lost during drying. So if the label says

with added vitamins

you are not always getting anything more than you would have had from the fresh food.

In some foods, though, you may get more nutrients in the convenience version than you do in the fresh. For example, vegetables lose their vitamin C content if they are left sitting around in the sun in the greengrocer's window, but if they are frozen they are taken straight from the fields to the freezer plant with scarcely any vitamin loss.

Should we eat convenience foods?

Convenience foods save time and effort, and we all want to do that sometimes. They can save us money, for example when we buy frozen foods in bulk, but sometimes they are more expensive. When you use convenience foods try to judge whether the time and effort saved is worth the cost, and whether the flavour is as good as the fresh or home-made version.

You could try a consumer test yourself

e.g. Compare a dehydrated beef risotto with a home-made beef risotto **or**

a packet bread mix with home-made bread **or**
fresh carrots with tinned or frozen carrots.

Make a table like this in which to fill in your results.

	Frozen chips	Home-made chips
Cost		
Time to make		
Other ingredients needed for convenience foods		
Flavour		
Colour		
Texture		
Conclusions		

Do you really know what you're eating when you buy a convenience food?

When you pick up a packet or tin of food there will probably be a label which will tell you something about the product – but do you know what it means?

Write down the meanings of these words used in food production. A dictionary may help.

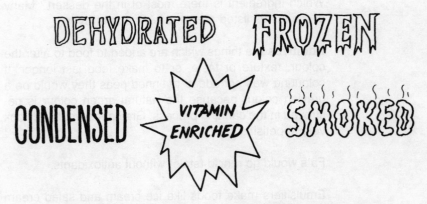

FOODFARE

Angel's chocolate dessert

Directions:
Put ½ pint cold milk into a basin
Sprinkle on the contents of this sachet, whisk thoroughly
Leave to thicken, turn into sundae glasses. Ready in 5 mins.
Eat same day or refrigerate overnight

Ingredients:
Sugar, Edible vegetable oil, Starch, Permitted Emulsifier, Sodium Caseinate, Lactose, Emulsifying Salts, Whey Powder, Flavourings, Lecithin, Sodium Aluminosilicate, Colour, Antioxidant

Average weight 71g.

Made by
Sweet Foods Ltd. London England

Here is the label for a chocolate dessert. What does the label tell you about this product? Does it tell you
how many servings it contains?
when it should be used by?

Could you understand the list of ingredients on the packet? The ingredients on a food packet must be listed in order with the one there is most of at the top. Which ingredient is there most of in the dessert? Many of the things listed are what we call **additives**.

Additives are things which are added to food to alter the colour, texture or taste, or to make food last longer. If colouring was not added to tinned peas they would be a greyish colour because the natural green colour is destroyed in the canning process. Grey peas would not look very appetising.

Fats would go rancid (stale) without antioxidants.

Emulsifiers make foods like ice cream and salad cream more creamy.

Sauces and soups are thickened by starch.

Sometimes nutrients are added to make a food more nutritious. Find out which nutrients are added to
flour
margarine

We should also be aware of what is in the fresh foods we eat.

3 kg potatoes can kill – this is because they contain the poison solenin. Green potatoes should never be eaten as they contain more solenin.

50 cups of strong coffee can cause caffeine poisoning. Just 5 cups can cause symptoms such as trembling and sleeplessness.

2 kg rhubarb can kill – this is because it contains oxalic acid, particularly in the leaves.

2 kg spinach can kill. This also contains oxalic acid.

It would be very difficult to eat or drink fatal amounts of these foods, but we should always be sensible about the amount of foods we eat!

Each year we eat about 1,200 g additives – that's about 12 aspirin-size tablets a week.

List the additives in the chocolate dessert on page 20.

Flavourings and colourings encourage us to eat too many convenience foods. Here is a list of some of the words used most often on food packets and their meanings. See if you can work out why each of the additives was added to the chocolate dessert.

agar (and extracts from it) is used for setting things

anti-oxidant prevents fruit from going brown and fats from becoming rancid

arrowroot comes from the root of a West Indian plant and is used for thickening

calcium lactate comes from milk. It is used to add a milk content to foods

calcium phosphate is a preservative and helps sugar to flow without lumps

caramel is a colouring

citric acid prevents oxidation (fruit going brown and fats rancid)

dextrose is sugar

emulsifier is a substance which is added to a mixture to prevent it from separating

enzyme is added to help something to happen, e.g. in cheese-making, rennet is added to milk to help it to set

extract is something which has been taken out of something else, e.g. beef extract is used in meat cubes

gelatine is made from the bones, skin and hooves of animals and is used to set things like jelly

hydrolise means to split up, e.g. fats are sometimes split up to make them more digestible

lecithin comes from egg whites and makes things creamy

monosodium glutamate has no taste itself but is added to bring out the flavour of foods like meat, fish and vegetables

niacin or **nicotinic acid** is a vitamin

riboflavin is the correct name for vitamin B2

sodium nitrite is a preservative

sodium phosphate is a preservative

soya bean is a plant from which we can obtain protein

starch is a white, tasteless powder found in rice, potatoes, etc., and is used to thicken things

sulphur dioxide is a preservative
tartaric acid prevents oxidation
thiamin is the correct name for vitamin B1
whey is the liquid produced when rennet is added to milk to make curds and whey. Remember Little Miss Muffet?

Collect some food labels from tins and packets you have at home. See if you can work out what is in them and why. Notice how often sugar and starch appear.

There are laws which protect consumers (a consumer is anyone who buys a product) when they buy food. Check one of your labels against the regulations shown below.

1

The law states that labels must be clear, informative and accurate and must carry a list of ingredients (except water) in order, with the one there is most of at the top.

2

There must be a description on the package that people will understand.

3

The package must contain the name and address of the packer, labeller or person in this country responsible for packing and labelling.

4

The name must be easily seen and the list of ingredients should be close to the name or in a box.

5

There must not be any misleading claim or advertisement on the label.

6

Foods which are dried must have the word 'dried' or 'dehydrated' on the packet.

7

Any convenience food which needs extra ingredients adding must list these on the packet.

8

When a food is flavoured it can only be called, for example 'raspberry yoghurt', if it has real raspberries in it rather than artificial raspberry flavouring. If the flavour is artificial the word 'flavour' must come straight after the food name in the same size letters.

If you buy a food which you think is breaking any of these laws you should take it to the local Trading Standards Department (usually found in the town hall) or Consumer Protection Department. The Citizens' Advice Bureau will tell you where to find them if you have any difficulty.

Take-away food

Some food is not only prepared, but also cooked for us. There are a growing number of take-away food shops where you can buy ready-cooked food to eat at home – fish and chip shops, Indian restaurants, Chinese restaurants and take-aways, etc.

1 Make a survey of the take-away food shops in your area. You could include

    type of food provided
    cost
    amount (e.g. number of chips, weight of rice)
    type of container provided (does it keep the
        food hot? is it grease resistant? is it hygienic?)
    how to order (on the spot, by telephone, etc.)
    time taken to prepare the food
    nutritional value (are there any nutrients
        missing?)

2 Make a survey of people in your class, school, street or home who use take-away food shops.
What questions would you ask them?

Convenience foods and take-away foods are all right as long as you don't live on them all the time and as long as you eat plenty of fresh green vegetables, wholemeal bread and fresh fruit as well.

Making food into meals

Try making a survey of the food eaten in a day or a week by your class, or by a few of your friends. Get them to write down everything they eat including drinks and snacks between meals. You will probably find that nobody eats exactly the same sort of food. We all have different diets. Look at these three diets for one day. Copy them into your books and answer the questions underneath.

Lazy Daisy
Breakfast: cup of coffee
Mid-morning: doughnut,
  coffee
Lunch: bag of crisps,
  chocolate biscuit, apple
Mid-afternoon: cup of tea
Tea: pork pie, orange
Evening: bag of chips

Slim Sue
Breakfast: orange juice,
  boiled egg, toast, coffee
Lunch: ham salad, orange,
  milk
Tea: lean pork chop, jacket
  potato, carrots, yoghurt
Evening: cup of black
  coffee

Fast Fred

Breakfast: cup of coffee, toast, cereal

Lunch: hamburger from take-away

Tea: frozen steak and kidney pie, tinned peas, chips, ice cream

Evening: beer, crisps

1 Who has the most fresh food in his/her diet?
2 Whose diet has the most convenience foods in it?
3 Who has to do the least work to get his/her meals?
4 Who do you think would spend the most money on his/her meals?
5 Whose meals would be quickest to prepare?
6 Whose meal is the most slimming?
7 Who is eating 'snacks' rather than 'meals'?
8 Whose diet has the most variety of foods?

Whether you are still at school, running a home, at work or a retired person, you still need a good variety of foods.

Adding up the additives

1 Can you recognise these foods from their list of ingredients?

a) Water, CO_2, sugar, saccharin, phosphoric acid, caffeine, cola bean extract.

b) Edible starch, flavourings, wheat flour, sugar, beef, salt, hydrolised vegetable protein, curry powder, oxtail, caramel, monosodium glutamate, yeast extract, tomato purée.

c) Sugar, edible vegetable oil with antioxidants, sodium caseinate, permitted emulsifier, starch, sodium phosphate, lecithin, flavourings, colour.

When you have thought about your answers, turn to page 123 and see if you are right.

2 Only one of these foods contains absolutely no additives. Do you know which it is?

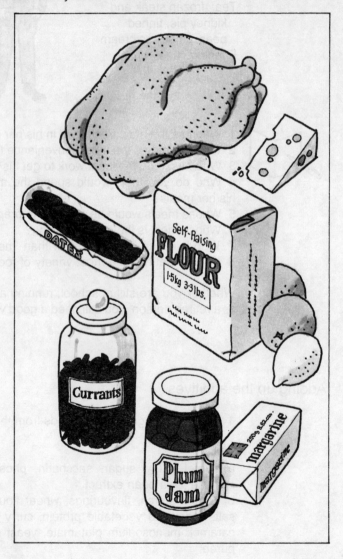

3 Have you got the energy?

One of the reasons the body needs food is to provide **energy** for everything we do.

We need energy for
    riding a bicycle...
    dressing...
    walking upstairs...
    swimming

Even when we are asleep or just sitting around doing nothing we need energy for things like heart beat, breathing and digestion.

We need energy for
    sleeping...
    watching TV

This need for energy is different for each of us depending on our
    age
    sex
    height
    weight
and is called our **basal metabolism**.

We measure the energy we need in **kilojoules**. Large numbers of kilojoules are measured in **megajoules**.
    1000 **kilojoules** = 1 **megajoule**

How many kilojoules do we need?

This is Jenny.

Eat to live

She is 14, 1.60 m (five feet three inches) tall and weighs 48.4 kg (seven stone two pounds). She needs 5023 kilojoules a day for her basal metabolism (just to keep going – even when asleep).

To find out how many more kilojoules she needs we will have to see how she spends her day.

7.30 Get up. Get washed, dressed	**8.00** Breakfast	**8.30** Walk to school	**9.00** Writing
10.00 Listening (30 min) Reading (30 min)	**11.00** Recreation	**11.15** Thinking (30 min) Writing (30 min)	**12.15** Lunch
12.45 Recreation	**1.30** Listening (30 min) Writing (30 min)	**2.30** Swimming	**3.30** Reading
4.00 Walk home	**4.30** Knitting	**5.30** Eating	**6.00** Homework – Writing
7.00 Watch TV	**10.30** Wash, undress	**11.00** Sleep	

We can make a kilojoule clock to show how many kilojoules are needed for each activity.

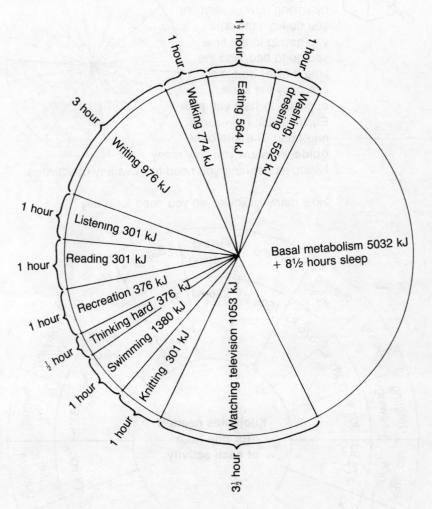

1 hour — Walking 774 kJ

1½ hour — Eating 564 kJ

1 hour — Washing, dressing, 552 kJ

3 hour — Writing 976 kJ

1 hour — Listening 301 kJ

1 hour — Reading 301 kJ

1 hour — Recreation 376 kJ

½ hour — Thinking hard 376 kJ

1 hour — Swimming 1380 kJ

1 hour — Knitting 301 kJ

3½ hour — Watching television 1053 kJ

Basal metabolism 5032 kJ + 8½ hours sleep

1 What is the total number of kilojoules Jenny needs for this day?

2 This is a school day. If it was the weekend what difference do you think this would make to the number of kilojoules Jenny needs?

3 Jenny walks to school. What difference do you think it would make if she went by bus?

Make up a kilojoule clock to
show your own day. Start
by writing down everything
you do from the time
you get up to the time
you go to bed, and the
time it takes you. You
can copy the circle
opposite to help you plan.
Each section represents
one hour. The **kilojoule
guide** will show you how many
kilojoules per hour you need for a variety of activities.

How many kilojoules do you need for a day?

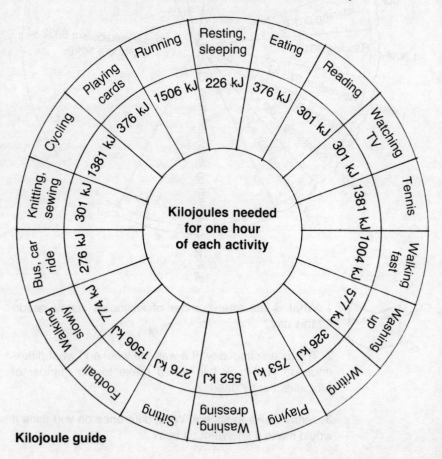

Kilojoule guide

Kilojoules needed for one hour of each activity

Playing cards — 376 kJ
Running — 1506 kJ
Resting, sleeping — 226 kJ
Eating — 376 kJ
Reading — 301 kJ
Watching TV — 301 kJ
Tennis — 1381 kJ
Walking fast — 1004 kJ
Washing up — 577 kJ
Writing — 326 kJ
Playing — 753 kJ
Washing, dressing — 552 kJ
Sitting — 276 kJ
Football — 1506 kJ
Walking slowly — 774 kJ
Bus, car ride — 276 kJ
Knitting, sewing — 301 kJ
Cycling — 1381 kJ

Look at these graphs which show the average weight and height of girls and boys from birth to age 20, and then answer the questions that follow.

Height in centimetres

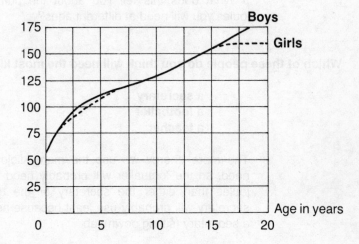

Weight in kilogrammes

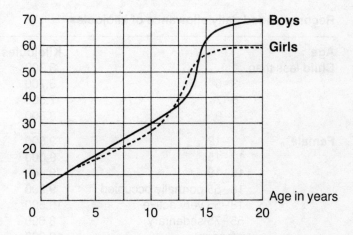

1 What is the average length and weight of a boy and girl at birth?

2 How much has the average child grown by the time he/she is five years old?

3 What do you notice about growth after the age of 15 or 16?

4 Is there any difference in the growth pattern for girls and boys?

5 What does this tell you about the number of kilojoules you will need at different ages?

Which of these people do you think will need the most kilojoules?

> **a secretary**
> **a footballer**
> **a teacher**

The more energy we use the more kilojoules we will need, so the footballer will probably need more megajoules than either the secretary or the teacher. The secretary will probably use least because he or she has a sedentary (sitting down) job.

Recommended daily allowance of kilojoules

Age		Kilojoules
Child less than	1	3,300
	3–5	6,700
	5–7	7,500
	7–9	8,800
Female	9–12	9,600
	12–15	9,600
	15–18	9,600
	18–55 normally occupied	9,200
	18–55 very active	10,500
	55–75 sedentary	8,600
	pregnant	10,000
Male	9–12	10,500
	12–15	11,700
	15–18	12,600
	18–35 sedentary	11,300
	18–35 moderately active	12,600
	18–35 very active	15,100
	35–75 sedentary	10,900

A table of recommended daily allowances has been worked out. This is a rough guide to the number of kilojoules needed by people of different ages every day – but remember, it is only a guide and will vary as you have seen depending on the type of day you spend.

Where do kilojoules come from?

We get our kilojoules from the food we eat. Most foods provide some kilojoules; some foods provide more kilojoules than others.

Which of these foods contains the most kilojoules?

1 teaspoon sugar   2 cm cube butter   1 slice ham

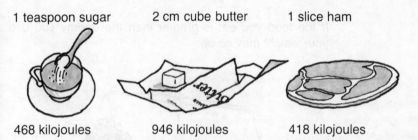

468 kilojoules   946 kilojoules   418 kilojoules

You will see that the butter – a fat – will give you twice as many kilojoules as the sugar or ham. So fatty foods provide the most kilojoules. This means not only fats like butter, margarine and oil, but also cream from the top of milk, fat on meat and oily fish.

Foods containing hardly any kilojoules
fruit
vegetables
Bovril

(Bananas, dates and dried fruits have more kilojoules than any other fruit.)

Can you have too many kilojoules?

If the food you eat is equal to the energy you use you should stay slim and fit.

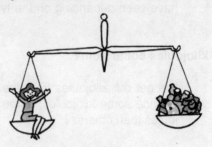

This is called **energy balance**.

If the food you eat is greater than the energy you use your weight may go up.

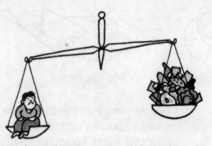

If the food you eat is less than the energy you use your weight may go down and you may become thin, tired and listless.

If you want to lose weight you must therefore either **eat less** or **use up more energy** without eating more. This is a slower process since exercise sometimes makes you more hungry.

The perils of not watching your energy balance

Daniel Lambert was born in Leicester in 1770. He weighed 203 kg by the time he was 23. When he died his body measured 3 metres round and his legs were a metre round. He weighed 327 kg at the time of his death and a wall had to be removed at the inn where he was staying so that the body could be removed.

If you are going to eat less, which foods are you going to cut down in your diet?

How could you use up more energy?

Look back at the kilojoule guide on page 32 to help you with your answer. It is never wise to go on a strict slimming diet without a doctor's advice, nor is it sensible to slim by cutting out food altogether. People who stop eating can end up suffering from a disease called **anorexia nervosa**. Because there is no food to provide energy the protein from their muscle tissue is used to provide energy instead, and they come unpleasantly thin.

If you do want to slim try to cut down on sugar, which you do not need, and fat rather than starch, and take more exercise.

What happens when we use up energy?

Try this experiment.

You will need a stopwatch or a watch with a second hand and a partner to help you.

Draw a table in your exercise book like the one below.

Use of energy

Body observations	Before exercise	After exercise	Increase
Pulse rate	/min	/min	/min
Breathing rate	/min	/min	/min
Does the forehead feel hotter/ cooler?			
Appearance of face (e.g. does it look pale or flushed?)			
Any other observations.			

1 Find the pulse in the wrist of your partner's hand by placing your fingers in the position shown below.

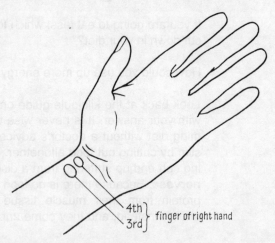

4th ⎫
3rd ⎭ finger of right hand

Count the number of pulse beats for one minute and write the results in your table.

2 Record the breathing rate by counting the number of times the chest rises and falls in a minute.

3 Test for temperature by placing your hand on your partner's forehead. Is it hotter, cooler or about the same as yours?

4 Check your partner's appearance. Note the colour of your partner's face and look for signs of perspiration.

5 Now tell your partner to run up and down some stairs or around the playground, or skip or do something else which is energetic for 4–5 minutes.

6 Immediately your partner stops, record the pulse rate and breathing rate.

7 Repeat steps 3 and 4 and fill in the table.

Can you suggest why the pulse rate and breathing rate change? Why do some people's faces appear pinker and why do they perspire more?

See how you're doing so far ...

So now you know about kilojoules. You know
> where we get them from
> how many we need
> how many other people need
> what we need them for
> how they are measured
> what happens if we have too many or too few

so let's see how much you can remember. (Answers are on pages 123–4.)

1 Which do you think would contain the most kilojoules per portion?
> **boiled potatoes**
> **jacket potatoes**
> **chips**
> **creamed potatoes**

2 Work out the total number of kilojoules in each of these meals.

Meal 1		kJ
beefburger	120 g	544
roll	120 g	837
onions	60 g	62
chips	120 g	1046
total		

Meal 2		kJ
milk	150 g	418
omelette	100 g	669
lettuce	20 g	0
cucumber	40 g	0
tomato	50 g	10
roll	30 g	343
butter	10 g	334
total		

Meal 3		kJ
doughnut	50 g	669
coffee (with milk and sugar)	200 g	276
total		

Which contains the most?
Which contains the least?

3 Keep a record of the kilojoules you consume in an average day. Compare this with the recommended daily allowance for your age and type. Use the kilojoule tables at the end of the chapter to help you with the calculations.

4 Which of these would you cut down or out if you were overweight?

cottage cheese	black coffee	bananas
Coca Cola	bread	apples
low fat yoghurt	cream	chips
treacle pudding	cucumber	dried milk

5 Arrange these people in order to show who would need the most kilojoules daily.

factory worker, six-month-old baby, welder, shop assistant, supermarket till operator, four-year-old girl, old man, pregnant woman

6 Arrange these activities in order to show which use up the most energy.

tennis, sitting, playing the violin, washing-up, football, digging the garden, running upstairs

1000 kilojoule (1 megajoule) portions

Fatty foods
olive oil	19 g
mayonnaise	30 g
butter	30 g
margarine	30 g
nuts (3 brazils, 12 almonds)	43 g
peanut butter	30 g
bacon	60 g
sardines in oil	88 g

Starchy foods
biscuits (2 sweet, 3 semi-sweet)	43 g
potatoes (boiled or jacket)	300 g
potatoes (chips)	88 g
crisps	60 g

bread	72 g
starch reduced bread	88 g
Energen rolls	60 g
Ryvita	60 g
cereals	60 g
flour	60 g
rice	60 g

Sweet foods

sugar	43 g
jam	88 g
syrup	88 g
honey	88 g
boiled sweets	60 g
ice cream	120 g
dried fruit (2 figs, 4 dates, 1 tablespoon of raisins)	43 g

Dairy foods

milk	150 ml
yoghurt	150 ml
cottage cheese	180 g
cheddar cheese	60 g
single cream	120 g
double cream	60 g

Meat and fish

ham	88 g
tongue	88 g
luncheon meat	148 g
poultry on the bone	180–240 g
poultry off the bone	120 g
plaice fillet	600 g
white fish fillet (frozen)	300 g

Pulses

dried pulses	480 g
cooked pulses	180 g
baked beans	240 g

Fruit and vegetables

bananas (unpeeled)	480 g
orange	720 g
apple	600 g

grapes	300 g
cabbage	1075 g
lettuce	1075 g
carrots	600 g
mushrooms	1675 g
frozen peas	300 g

Drinks

sherry	2 small glasses
wine	2 small tumblers
stout	2 small tumblers
spirits	2 measures

The following foods contain practically no kilojoules

all green vegetables
radishes
cucumber
gherkins
tomato juice
consommé
olives
meat and yeast extract (Bovril and Marmite)

4 Fit for fibre

Take some brown and some white flour and sieve a little of each onto a plate. Describe what is left in the sieve and what is on the plate in each case.

The brown grain in the sieve is **bran**. It is the part of our diet which we call **fibre**.

Without fibre we can suffer from constipation, and a constant shortage may even lead to bowel cancer, piles and diverticulitis (a serious inflammation).

Some people sprinkle bran on their food or take tablets to make sure they have enough fibre, but you can get fibre naturally by eating these foods.

Cereals
wholemeal bread, flour
oats
soya flour
rye biscuits

Vegetables
beans, peas, corn
mung beans

Nuts

Fruit
dried fruits
berry fruits (e.g. blackberries)
apricots

Breakfast Cereals
bran cereals
    (All-bran, muesli, bran flakes, etc.)
porridge

Eating brown or wholemeal bread is one of the easiest ways of adding fibre to your diet.

> **Wholemeal flour** contains 100 per cent of the grain (none of the bran is taken away).
> **Wholemeal bread** is 9 per cent fibre.

> Other **brown flour** contains 70–95 per cent of the whole grain.
> Other **brown breads** are 5 per cent fibre.

> **White flour** has nearly all the bran removed.
> **White bread** is 3 per cent fibre.

Try ordinary brown bread before wholemeal if you have only ever eaten white bread before. Then try switching to wholemeal. Switching to wholemeal means fewer kilojoules (important if you are trying to lose weight). Weight for weight, there are 900 kilojoules in 100 g wholemeal bread and 975 kilojoules in 100 g white. If you are trying to slim it is particularly important not to cut out all the starchy foods which contain fibre. Slimmers often suffer from constipation because of this. Try cutting down on fats and sugar instead.

Eating breakfast cereals is another way of adding fibre to your diet, but you need to know which are the ones which contain the most fibre. Arrange these breakfast cereals in order to show which you think contain the most fibre. The more wheatbran there is, the more fibre there will be in the cereal.

Sugar Puffs	Weetabix
porridge oats	Wholemeal Shreddies
cornflakes	Bran Buds
All-bran	Puffed Wheat
Rice Crispies	Readybrek
Shredded Wheat	Special K
Swiss breakfast	Sugar Smacks
cereal (e.g. Alpen)	

Now turn to page 124 to see if you are right. Copy the list in the correct order into your book.

If you are uncertain about changing your diet in any of these ways, start by replacing one-third or one-half of the white flour in recipes with brown. You may find that recipes need a little more liquid when using brown flour.

To increase the amount of fibre in your diet what could you replace each of the following by? Look back at page 45 if you are not sure.

> white bread by
> Rice Crispies by
> cream crackers by

Using more vegetables is another way of adding fibre to your diet. Vegetables like peas and beans contain protein too, so you could cut down on the meat in a casserole or stew when you add vegetables, and save money as well as adding fibre.

Bean sprouts are one vegetable which is a good source of fibre. You may be familiar with them in Chinese food. You can grow your own to use in meat dishes or salads.

How to grow your own bean sprouts

 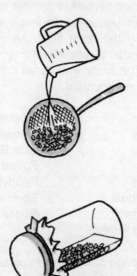 

This method will produce tasty bean sprouts ready to eat in 5–7 days.

1 Rinse 2–4 tablespoons mung bean seeds in tepid (just warm) water and put in a large jar (a coffee jar is ideal).

2 Add just enough water to cover the beans and cover the jar with muslin held in place with a rubber band.

3 Place the jar on its side in a warm place.

4 Every morning and evening drain off the water through the muslin, add enough water to cover the seeds again and place the jar on its side.

5 When the mung beans have sprouts 2–4 cm long they are ready to use.

6 Tip them out of the jar and rinse them to remove husks.

7 Serve cooked with rice or add raw to salads.

Try to remember these ways of adding fibre to your diet, and try them out.

Eat more bread, especially wholemeal or brown.
Eat more potatoes, especially jacket potatoes so that you eat the skins.
Have a high fibre cereal for breakfast.
Eat plenty of vegetables, especially green leafy vegetables, beans and salads.
Eat plenty of fresh fruit.

Recipes for a few dishes which contain fibre

Brown bread rolls (8 rolls)

100 g strong, brown flour
100 g strong, plain white flour
1 level teaspoon salt
1 level teaspoon granulated sugar
10 g margarine
12 g fresh yeast *or* 2 level teaspoons dried yeast
75 ml hot water
75 ml cold milk

Method

1 Put the oven on at regulo 6 (400° F or 200° C).
2 Grease baking tray.
3 Sieve flour and salt into a mixing bowl. Rub margarine into flour.
4 Mix the hot water and cold milk together.
5 Place the yeast and sugar in a small basin and add a little of the warm liquid.
6 Add the yeast mixture to the flour, by making a hole in the middle of the flour and pouring it in.
7 Beat with a wooden spoon and add enough of the rest of the liquid to make a soft dough.
8 Turn out onto the table and knead for 5 minutes.
9 Make into 8 rolls and place on baking tray.
10 Place in a warm place for at least 20 minutes.
11 Cook in the middle of the oven for 15–20 minutes until golden brown.

Pork with bean sprouts (for one)

50 g long grain rice
150 g pork fillet
1 tablespoon oil
1–2 dessertspoons soy sauce
2 sticks celery
50 g mushrooms
½ stock cube
75 g bean sprouts
1 tinned pineapple ring

2–3 tablespoons pineapple syrup
1 dessertspoon cornflour
100 ml water

Method
1 Chop the pork. Wash and chop the mushrooms and celery. Chop the pineapple.
2 Bring a saucepan of water to the boil. Add the bean sprouts. Bring the water back to the boil, then drain the bean sprouts and put them into cold water. Drain them thoroughly.
3 In a large saucepan fry the pork in the oil for 3–5 minutes.
4 Add the mushrooms and celery and cook gently for 5 minutes.
5 Mix the cornflour with the pineapple juice. Add 100 ml water.
6 Add to the pan and bring to the boil, stirring all the time.
7 Add the stock cube, bean sprouts and pineapple.
8 Cook for 5 minutes or until meat is tender.
9 Put rice into a pan of boiling water. Cook gently for 15–20 minutes. Drain and serve.

Fruit and oat slices (12 slices)

100 g plain flour
50 g wholemeal flour
100 g oats
100 g brown sugar
125 g margarine
300 g dates, raisins, apricots or a mixture of all three

Method
1 Put oven on regulo 5 (375° F or 190° C).
2 Grease a 17.5 cm square, shallow tin.
3 Put the fruit into a bowl and cover with boiling water.
4 Put all the other ingredients into a mixing bowl and rub the fat in.
5 Put half the mixture into the tin. Press it down firmly.
6 Drain the fruit and spread it in the tin.

7 Cover with the rest of the mixture. Press down firmly once more.
8 Cook for 40–50 minutes until crisp and brown.
9 Cut into 12 fingers while still hot, but leave in the tin until cool.

Breakfast cereal (for two)

> 2 rounded tablespoons oats
> 2½ tablespoons milk
> 1 teaspoon honey
> 100 g fresh fruit
> juice of ½ orange or a tablespoon blackcurrant or rose-hip syrup
> chopped nuts

1 Soak the oats overnight in milk.
2 Before serving, add the rest of the ingredients plus more milk if liked.

5 The fats of life

What do you know about fats?

At the end of this chapter, on pages 67–8, you will find a quiz about **fats.** Turn to this now and see how many of the answers you know or can guess. Then work through the chapter. When you have done this you should be able to fill in any gaps, or correct your answers.

What is fat?

We call all of these fat, but when we talk about FAT in relation to food we mean the sort of fat shown in pictures 2 and 3.

We can divide the fat in foods into two types.

Visible fats are the fats or oils you can see, which are bought and used in cooking, or eaten as they are.

Invisible fats are eaten in foods which contain fat.

You *can* see some of them, for example, the fat on meat or cream on milk. You will only know if others are there by reading the food label or by doing the following simple test.

To test if a food contains fat, take a sample from one of the following foods.

Rub the food on a sheet of white paper.

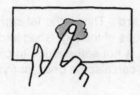

Now hold the paper up to the light.

If the food contains fat, you will see a bright spot on the paper where it has become **translucent**.

translucent spot
(allows light to show through)

Find six different foods to test yourself and make a table in your book like the one below. Fill in the results of your own tests.

Food	Observation

What kind of wrapping is used for fats?
Why do think this is?

What are fats made from?

Oil	Cooking oil may be made from olives, maize, cotton seed, groundnuts, soya beans, rape seeds, or sunflower seeds. If the bottle says 'blended oils' it means that more than one of these has been used. Oil is used mainly for frying foods. It does not hold the flavour of food that has been cooked in it, if it is strained after use. Olive oil is the most expensive. Some people think it has the best flavour. It is more often used for salad dressings than cooking in this country.

Lard	This is the fat surrounding the kidneys and intestines of the pig. Good lard is pure white with little flavour. It is not soft enough to cream, but it makes pastry crisp. It can also be used for frying.

Suet	This is prepared from the fat found around the kidneys of beef cattle or sheep. It is very hard and cannot be rubbed into flour or creamed. It is added to foods by being finely chopped and stirred in. Prepared suet, bought in a packet, is already shredded and mixed with wheat or rice flour to stop it sticking together. It is used mainly for steamed dishes, e.g. puddings, pies and dumplings, and it can be baked, but this makes food dry.

Dripping	This is the savoury fat which drips from roast meat during cooking. It is eaten on bread and used for frying meat when making casseroles and other meat dishes.

Butter	Butter is made by churning cream which has been removed from milk. Cows' milk is used. It takes the cream from 18 pints (over ten litres) of milk to make about 400 g butter. It is used when a good flavour is wanted on bread or toast, and can be used in cakes, biscuits and buttercream.

Margarine	This was first made as a substitute for butter. It is made from oils which are blended together. The oils used are from groundnuts, cotton seed, palm trees, coconut, soya and whale. Milk, salt and vitamins A and D are added. The vitamins increase the nutritional value of margarine. Soft margarines are whipped so that they include more air and are easier to cream. Low calorie margarines have water added and do not contain as much fat. Because of this they are not suitable for cooking with. They would make a hard, dry pastry. Some margarines are low in cholesterol, which means they contain less of the substance which clogs up the arteries in the body and can lead to heart disease.

Cooking fat This costs the same as margarine and is made from the same, partly-hardened oils as margarine, but without trying to imitate butter, so no colourings or vitamins are added. Some are creamed and have air beaten in.

Copy this table into your book and fill in the right hand column.

Margarine is made from

Lard is made from

Butter is made from

Suet is made from

Cooking oil is made from

Cooking fat is made from

Dripping is made from

The uses of fats in cooking

These are all fats which are used in cooking. Draw or list them in your book.

olive oil   dripping
margarine   butter
cooking fat   polyunsaturated margarine
lard   suet
super soft margarine   blended vegetable oil

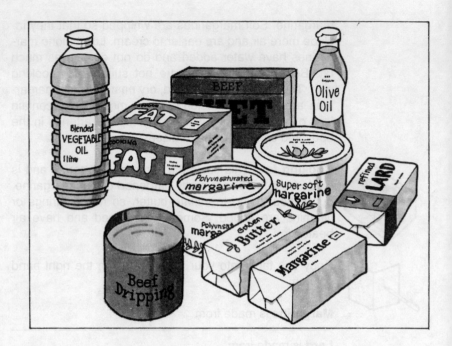

Find out the approximate cost of 250 g of each fat and add this to your list.

Now copy the table below into your book and complete the column on the right.

Which fat would you use for making

pastry
___

salad dressing
___

dumplings
___

cakes ('one-stage' mixture)
___

frying chips
___

spreading on bread
___

greasing tins

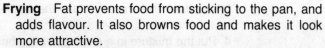

The main uses of fats in cooking

Frying Fat prevents food from sticking to the pan, and adds flavour. It also browns food and makes it look more attractive.

Shortening It is the fat in pastry which makes it crisp and crumbly.

Holding air Fat holds in the air which is beaten into cakes during mixing.

Greasing tins This prevents the food from sticking to the tin when you try to get it out.

'One-stage' mixtures Soft fats, which cream easily, can be mixed directly with other dry ingredients, saving preparation time.

Basting Spooning fat over roasted meat or other food keeps it moist during cooking.

Making emulsions The following experiments will help you to understand what an **emulsion** is. You will need a magnifying glass.

French dressing

Collect
75 ml malt vinegar
150 ml oil
¼ teaspoon salt
pinch pepper
screw top jar
watch or clock with second hand
egg whisk
magnifying glass

1 Put the vinegar in the jar with the salt and pepper. Shake well. Pour in the oil and leave the jar to stand for 1 minute.
Where does the oil go?

2 Cover the jar and shake it about ten times, then let it stand. Time how long it takes for the oil and vinegar to separate.

3 Shake the jar different numbers of times and look at

the mixture closely (with a magnifying glass) immediately after shaking.
When does the dressing have the smallest droplets?

4 Put the mixture in a small bowl and beat it hard for two minutes Pour it back into the jar and examine it closely.
How long does the dressing take to separate into two layers? What did shaking and beating do to the size of the droplets?

The mixture of oil and vinegar you have made is an **emulsion**. It will not stay mixed together, so it must be made immediately before it is used. Emulsions can be made to **stabilise** – stay mixed together. In mayonnaise the oil and vinegar mixture is stabilised by adding egg yolk.

How much fat do you eat?

Make a list of all the foods you ate yesterday. Underline all the fats. (Remember the **visible** and **invisible** fats.)

If you read food labels, you may discover that you eat more fat than you think.

Collect some food labels of your own and stick them into your book. Underline any fats mentioned.

Do you know why fats are used so often in convenience foods?

Do we need fats?

Fats provide vitamins A and D. They are added to margarine by law to make sure that we have enough. If children do not have enough vitamin D when they are growing they may develop a disease called **rickets**, which causes bowed legs. But as green vegetables and carrots contain vitamin A, and more than enough vitamin D can be absorbed from sunlight on the skin, we should still limit our intake of fats. A large amount of the fat we eat comes from animal sources e.g. dairy produce and meat and lard. This fat is called **Saturated fat** and it can increase the amount of **cholesterol** in the blood stream, leading to blockage of the arteries and heart disease. **Polyunsaturated** fats contain some of the essential fats the body needs and are found in vegetable oils and fats and some fish. Eating some polyunsaturated fats may help to reduce cholesterol.

What happens if we eat too much fat?

We get fat or obese. About half the people in this country weigh more than is good for them. Obesity not only looks and feels unpleasant but obese people are likely to be more prone to heart disease, high blood pressure, angina, diabetes and problems in pregnancy.

How can you tell if you are too fat?

1 Check your weight against the chart below.

Height and weight chart

(This is an approximate guide only. Individual builds vary greatly.)

Age	Height (metres)	Weight (kg)
Girls		
1–2	0.81	10.8
2–3	0.91	13.6
3–5	1.04	16.3
5–7	1.14	20.3
7–9	1.35	31.2
9–12	1.42	33.0
12–15	1.60	48.4
15–18	1.63	55.7
Boys		
1–2	0.81	10.8
2–3	0.91	13.6
3–5	1.04	16.3
5–7	1.14	20.3
7–9	1.35	31.2
9–12	1.40	33.0
12–15	1.58	48.4
15–18	1.73	55.7

2 Weight is not always an accurate guide to fat. Some people have greater muscle development which adds to their weight. A better way to test if you are overweight is to pinch the skin at the back of your arm, with the tip of your forefinger and thumb, halfway between the shoulder and elbow, holding your arm down.

If the fold of skin is more than an inch thick you are very fat.

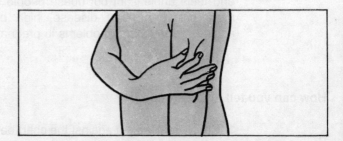

Heart disease

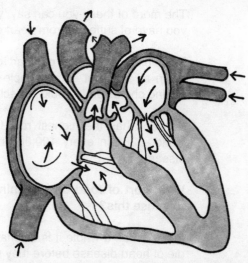

Heart disease is caused when blood cannot get through to the muscles that make up the wall of the heart. The arteries that take blood to these muscles have become blocked. The arteries are blocked by a build up of **cholesterol**, a fatty substance found in the blood, and other substances. We all have cholesterol in our bodies, made by the liver. Some foods we eat also produce a lot of cholesterol in the blood. Cholesterol is found in foods of animal origin.

Foods high in cholesterol	Foods low in cholesterol
animals fats (lard, suet, dripping, butter)	vegetable fats (margarine, oil)
eggs	skimmed milk
offal (liver, kidneys, etc.)	yoghurt (low fat)
cream, milk	cottage cheese
shell fish, oily fish	white fish
fried and roasted foods	grilled or boiled foods

There are many things which increase the chance of heart disease. These include

> **high blood pressure**
> **smoking**
> **lack of exercise**
> **obesity**
> **family history of heart disease**
> **stress**
> **eating too much saturated fat**

The more of these you can say 'yes' to, the more chance you have of suffering from heart disease.

To avoid the chance of heart disease you should cut down all fats, but some people believe that those containing cholesterol should especially be avoided.

Scotland has the highest rate for heart disease in the world – 365 in every 100,000 deaths are due to heart disease.

What sort of food do you think is eaten in Scotland to cause this?

In Britain as a whole it is estimated that 55,000 men will die of heart disease before they reach retiring age.

How can we help ourselves to be fit not fat?

We should all cut down our fat consumption by a quarter. If we are obese we need to cut down more than this.

What could we replace the following foods with in our diet in order to cut down on fats? (Answers on page 125.)

We could replace
animal fats

                    by

We could replace full
cream milk

                    by

We could replace
hard cheeses

                    by

We could replace blended oils

by

We could replace frying

by

We could replace roasting

by

We could replace oily fish

by

We could replace cream

by

We could also cut down by

 cutting fat off meat

 not buttering vegetables

 roasting meat on a trivet so that fat drips off

 omitting the pre-frying of vegetables

 cooking in foil

Remember also when you pick a pudding that one containing sugar is fattening; one containing fat and sugar is very fattening.

Try some of these recipes, which replace the fats you would normally use with those containing less cholesterol – the polyunsaturated fats. If someone can make the standard recipe you could compare the results. Make a chart like the one below to fill in your results.

	Appearance	Flavour	Texture	Other Comments
Standard recipe				
Polyunsatuated recipe				

Conclusion (which you prefer, and your reasons why)

Victoria Sandwich (using polyunsaturated margarine)

125 g self-raising flour
1 level teaspoon baking powder
125 g polyunsaturated margarine
125 g caster sugar
2 eggs
2 tablespoons jam
few drops of vanilla essence

Method
1 Put oven on regulo 4 (350° F or 180° C).
2 Grease the bottoms of two 17.5 cm sandwich tins and line them with greaseproof paper.
3 Sieve the flour, baking powder and salt into a bowl and stir in the sugar.
4 Add the oil, eggs, milk and vanilla essence and beat well until the mixture becomes creamy.
5 Divide the mixture between the tins and bake for 30 minutes.
6 When cool, sandwich the two halves together with jam.

Short crust pastry 1 (using polyunsaturated vegetable oil)

135 g plain flour
1 level teaspoon caster sugar
pinch salt
4 tablespoons vegetable oil
2 tablespoons skimmed milk

Method

1 Put the oven on regulo 7 (425° F or 220° C).
2 Sieve the flour and salt into a 17.5 cm flan dish. Add the sugar.
3 Whisk the oil and milk together and pour all of it onto the flour. Mix with a fork to a manageable dough.
4 Press the pastry round the flan case.
5 Prick all over and bake for 15 minutes.

Shortcrust Pastry 2 (using polyunsaturated vegetable oil)

5 tablespoons vegetable oil
3 tablespoons water
175 g plain flour
pinch salt

Method

1 Put oven on regulo 7 (425° F or 220° C).
2 Sieve the flour and salt together.
3 Whisk the oil and water together and pour all at once onto the flour.
4 Mix with a fork to a manageable dough.
5 Roll out between sheets of greaseproof or non-stick paper, without extra flour.
6 Peel off the top paper. Place the pastry in a 17.5 cm flan dish with the paper side up. Peel the paper off.
7 Cook for 15 minutes.

Short Crust Pastry 3 (using polysaturated margarine)

100 g polyunsaturated margarine
15 ml water
175 g plain flour

Method
1 Put the oven on regulo 6 (400° F or 200° C).
2 Place the margarine, water and one third of the flour in a mixing bowl and cream the ingredients with a fork until they are well mixed.
3 Stir in the remaining flour to form a firm dough.
4 Turn onto a lightly floured surface and knead well until the dough is smooth.
5 Roll the dough out and line a plate with it.
6 Cook for 20 minutes.

All-in-one white sauce (using polyunsaturated margarine and skimmed milk)

25 g polyunsaturated margarine
25 g flour
300 ml skimmed milk (made with skimmed milk powder)
salt and pepper to taste

Method
1 Place all the ingredients in a saucepan.
2 Bring to the boil gently, stirring continuously.
3 Cook for 2–3 minutes until the sauce is thick and smooth.

Mayonnaise (using egg white and polyunsaturated vegetable oil)

¼ teaspoon sugar
½ teaspoon dry mustard
¼ teaspoon salt
4 teaspoons vinegar or lemon juice
1 egg white
200 ml sunflower oil

Method
1 Put the sugar and seasonings into a small bowl. Add the vinegar or lemon juice.
2 Beat the egg white until it is thick but not stiff, using a rotary beater.
3 Add half of the oil a little at a time, beating after each addition.

4 Continue beating while adding the blended vinegar.
5 Add the remaining oil gradually.
6 Chill the mayonnaise well.

What do you know about fats?

1 How much fat do you think is eaten per week in an average family?
> **50 g**
> **600 g**
> **100 g**

2 It takes the cream from
> a) **18 pints** (about 10 litres)
> b) **2 pints** (about 1 litre)
> c) **10 pints** (about 5 litres)

of milk to make 400 g butter.

3 Which country has the highest incidence of heart disease in the world?
> **Japan**
> **America**
> **Scotland**

4 Which margarine is the best for slimmers?
> **low cholesterol** margarine
> **soft** margarine
> **low kilojoule** margarine

5 Which of these contain fat?
> **chocolate**
> **cheese**
> **oranges**
> **sardines**
> **bread**

6 Which of the following meals would you choose if you were trying to cut down on fats?
> **Roast chicken, roast potatoes, peas Yorkshire pudding,**
> **Spaghetti bolognese**
> **Grilled lamb chop, boiled potatoes, carrots**

> **Steak and kidney pie, boiled potatoes, runner beans**
> **Ham salad**

7 Arrange these foods in order of expense with the most expensive at the top.

> **margarine**
> **suet**
> **butter**
> **olive oil**
> **lard**

8 Which vitamins does margarine contain?

> **B2**
> **C**
> **D**
> **A**
> **B1**

9 Which of these are vegetable fats?

> **oil**
> **lard**
> **butter**
> **margarine**
> **suet**

10 Carry out a survey of fats and oils in your local supermarket. Find out which contain saturated and which polyunsaturated fat.

(Answers on page 125).

6 Does it matter how much sugar we eat?

A hundred years ago the average person in Britain probably ate little more than 2 kg sugar in a whole year. Today we each consume on average 50 kg a year.

How?

In tea, coffee or other milk drinks

In ice creams, ice lollies, cakes, jam and drinks

In sweets and chocolates

Even in tinned foods like meat, soup or peas

Look at these food labels. Copy them into your book and underline any sugar mentioned.

Why do you think sugar is included in so many foods?

Make a collection of labels from foods you have at home, and underline the sugar in these. Next time you eat any of these foods try and taste the sugar for yourself.

If you are not sure whether a food contains sugar there is a simple test you can do. Try it first with a few foods that you know contain sugar.

Test for simple sugars

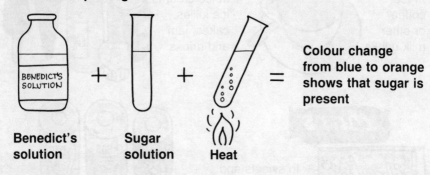

Benedict's solution + **Sugar solution** + **Heat** = Colour change from blue to orange shows that sugar is present

Why do you think things were so different 100 years ago?

One of the reasons why we eat so much sugar now is that we are encouraged to eat sweet foods from the time we are babies. Mothers add sugar to baby foods thinking that the baby will prefer the taste, but in fact a baby is used to milk which has a bland (mild) taste and would quite happily accept foods without sugar. Once the baby has tasted it, sugar becomes addictive – try giving it up yourself!

Don't give a baby sweetened foods or drinks.
Don't give children sweets as a present.
Don't give a baby a sweetened dummy to suck for hours.

If you do, you will help the baby to become fat, and this may slow its development – it is harder to crawl and walk when you are carrying a lot of weight around.

And what about you?

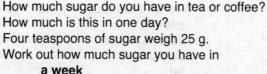

How much sugar do you have in tea or coffee?
How much is this in one day?
Four teaspoons of sugar weigh 25 g.
Work out how much sugar you have in
>   **a week**
>   **a month**
>   **a year**
How many kilojoules is this?

How much sugar do we need?

Well, sugar is the one thing which we can safely leave out of our diet. So many foods contain it that it is impossible to go without it completely.

Now make a list of all the things **you** eat which contain or are cooked in sugar, e.g. biscuits and fruit.

You may not have a weight problem now, but if you eat too much sugar you could have, later in life, together with dental trouble, heart disease and diabetes.

Do you eat sweets?

25 g sugar provides 420 kilojoules. Sweets are almost 100 per cent sugar, so to use up the kilojoules given by 25 g sweets you would have to

**walk briskly for
22.5 minutes**   **or run for
11 minutes**

**or dig for
20 minutes**   **or swim for
11 minutes**

on top of your normal activity or the sugar will be laid down in the body as fat.

Would you really do all this?

What is all this sugar doing for you?

This is what one tablespoon of sugar contains.

energy	668 kilojoules
carbohydrate	44 g
calcium	0
fat	0
protein	0
iron	0
vitamin A	0
vitamin D	0
thiamin	0
riboflavin	0
ascorbic acid	0

 Explain in your own words the nutritional value of sugar. We say sugar has **empty kilojoules** as it contains nothing much but kilojoules.

What happens when we have too much sugar?

1 Too many kilojoules make us fat or obese

Since sugar is providing nothing but kilojoules it should be the first food to be banned from your diet if you are slimming.

If you are overweight, not only will you have difficulty finding clothes to fit and suffer embarassment, but you will also be more likely to have varicose veins, foot trouble, back-ache, arthritis, gallstones, high blood pressure, heart attacks, strokes and diabetes.

2 **Too much sugar rots our teeth**

Tooth decay or **dental caries** is caused by **plaque**. Plaque is composed of bacteria, from our saliva and from tiny pieces of food lodged in our teeth, and is deposited on our teeth. When sugar comes in contact with it, acid is formed which attacks the surface of the enamel and forms a hole. The decay gets in further and enlarges the hole, and may also cause gum disease.

Tooth showing decay spreading

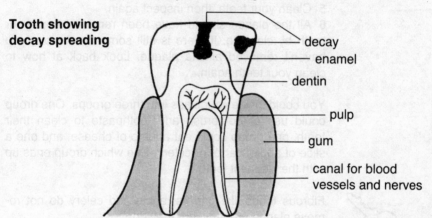

- decay
- enamel
- dentin
- pulp
- gum
- canal for blood vessels and nerves

The only way to remove plaque is to clean your teeth correctly.

Cleaning the teeth properly – this should take three minutes

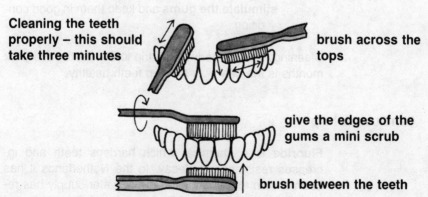

brush across the tops

give the edges of the gums a mini scrub

brush between the teeth

You can find out whether you are cleaning your teeth properly by using **disclosing tablets**. These will colour any plaque in your mouth bright red or bright blue. You can buy them from most chemists.

Try this experiment

1 Put a little vaseline on your lips. This will prevent them from being stained with the dye from the tablet.
2 Chew a disclosing tablet well and rinse round your mouth.
3 Spit the remainder of the tablet out and rinse your mouth with water.
4 Look in the mirror and see where the stain is.
5 Clean your teeth, then inspect again.
6 All the plaque should have been removed from your teeth by cleaning. If there is still some dye visible, you haven't removed all the plaque. Look back at how to clean your teeth again.

You could divide your class into three groups. One group could use a toothbrush and toothpaste to clean their teeth, one group could eat a lump of cheese, and one a slice of apple, carrot or celery. See which group ends up with the cleanest teeth.

Fibrous foods like carrots, apple and celery do not remove plaque properly, but they do
remove bits of debris from between the teeth
stimulate the saliva which helps to neutralise the acid in the mouth
stimulate the gums and keep them in good condition.

Cleaning teeth properly and a trip to the dentist every six months is the only way to keep teeth healthy.

Can fluoride help?

Fluoride is a chemical which hardens teeth and increases resistance to decay. In the Netherlands it has been shown that fluoridation of the water supply has reduced dental decay by 50 per cent and the number of extractions by 85 per cent. Fluoride is added to the water in some areas, but not everyone agrees that this should be done. It can be bought in tablet form and you can also use a fluoride toothpaste.

What happens to the sugar we eat?

Any sugar we eat dissolves in our **saliva**. It then passes through the stomach into the **small intestine**, where it is digested and passed into the blood.

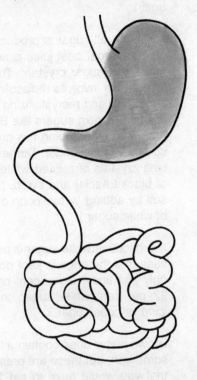

Any sugar which is not needed for energy is stored as fat. To be stored it has to be removed from the blood. This is done by the **pancreas** which produces just enough of a chemical called **insulin** to remove the extra sugar. You may have heard of the pancreas before. Animal pancreases are bigger than ours and are sold as **sweetbreads**.

Diabetes is a disease which people suffer from when the body does not produce enough insulin to deal with the extra sugar, so that the sugar stays in the blood. The body then gets clogged with sugar and the muscles cannot work. Diabetics have to get their supply of insulin artificially by injections or tablets or follow a special diet to control their sugar levels.

Brown sugar or white?

Should we be choosing brown sugar or white? Well, brown sugar is about twice as expensive as white, and Barbados or Muscovado sugar is almost twice as much again.

However, all sugar is produced in the same way. Sugar cane or sugar beet juice is added to water and boiled to make raw sugar crystals. These crystals then need refining. This involves redissolving the sugar in water, concentrating and recrystallizing over and over again until it is white. Brown sugars like Barbados or Muscovado are produced by stopping this process before the sugar becomes white. London Demerara sugar is made by tossing crystals of refined white sugar in molasses (a kind of black treacle) and syrup. (You can do the same yourself by adding ¼ teaspoon of black treacle to half a cup of white sugar.)

It is because white sugar is produced in such large quantities that the price is kept down. Tate and Lyle produce only just under 2 per cent brown or Demerara sugar to 92 per cent white sugar, the remainder being caster, icing or cube sugar.

Brown sugar does contain a little vitamin B1 and B2 and some iron, but these are present in such small quantities that you would have to eat 110 g a day to provide you with only one-sixtieth of your daily requirement of the vitamins and one-twentieth of the iron you need. This would also provide you with 1672 kilojoules so you would end up very fat if you relied on sugar to provide these.

How can you cut down sugar consumption?

1 Give up sugar in tea or coffee, or cut down.
2 If you have a weight problem and cannot take drinks without sugar use a sweetener like Sucron, Sweetex, Hermesetas or saccharine (which is sweeter than sugar but contains no kilojoules) and use sweeteners for cooking too.

3 Think about what you are eating. Which of these would be best for a mid-morning snack?

4 Try not to eat between meals and eat only when you can clean your teeth afterwards.

5 If you must eat sweets have them at only one time in the day, when you can clean your teeth afterwards.

6 Always clean your teeth last thing at night.

How sweet are you?

Answer the following questions in your book.

1 Unscramble these words.

a) The effects of eating too much sugar.

TBESOIY   ENDTLA ACIRES   IDBASTEE

b) Types of sugar

INCGI   ARBBDOAS   OSFT BONWR

ARREDMEA   LAGNRADETU

EUBC   ASCRTE   OUCVMSDAO

2 Fill in the blanks.

a) Sugar provides . . . . kilojoules because it provides us with . . . . and only adds . . . . to the diet.

b) If we do not clean our teeth the . . . . which builds up will cause . . . . and . . . . will attack the . . . . forming a hole which will need . . . . If it is left too long . . . . may be necessary. This can be prevented by . . . . and visiting the dentist every . . . .

(Answers on pages 125–6.)

7 Building for the future

Protein, as you may remember from Chapter 1, is needed to build and repair the body.

Calcium is needed for building bones and teeth and iron is needed for making blood.

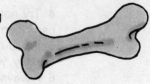

It is important to include all three of these building materials in our diet throughout our lives. They are especially necessary for children and young people when they are growing, and for pregnant women.

Protein

Some of our protein comes from animal foods. Approximately 50 g protein is supplied by 175 g cheese, 8 eggs, 175 g meat, 3 pints milk, 250 g fish.

Some of our protein comes from vegetable foods. Approximately 50 g protein is supplied by 700 g (3 large tins) peas, 900 g beans, 175 g nuts (e.g. peanuts), 325 g oats, 750 g lentils, 600 g bread.

The vegetable foods do not provide such a good form of protein as the animal foods. Some protein in our foods should come from the animal foods and some from the vegetable foods. They are often eaten together — bread and cheese for example. There is one group of people for whom this would not be possible — strict vegetarians.

Vegetarians who do not eat meat, eggs, milk or cheese for religious or health reasons must plan their diets carefully.

Lacto vegetarians do not eat meat, but they will eat milk, cheese and eggs, so they still get a good supply of protein.

Strict vegetarians or **vegans** can only eat the vegetable foods which contain protein. They will need to eat a great variety of these foods to get enough protein.

How much protein do we need?

This varies depending on our age, sex and weight.
Girls and women need 50–63 g daily
Boys and men need 60–90 g daily

If you include some protein foods in every meal, and make sure you have some animal and some vegetable foods containing protein every day, you will probably have enough.

Can we have too much protein?

Most people eat twice as much protein as they need. Why is this extravagant? This won't make them any stronger or healthier and the extra protein will just be used as an energy food. Moreover, a high meat consumption has been linked with large bowel cancer.

Think of the other foods which supply energy.

Can we have too little protein?

In Great Britain we have a good supply of protein foods, so people frequently get more protein than they need. Protein foods do tend to be expensive though so elderly people or people with low incomes could go short.

Remember that
eggs
cheese
bread
cereals
peas
and **beans**
are cheaper sources of protein than meat and fish.

In poorer countries where there is not such a good supply of protein foods, children who don't get enough protein may suffer from a disease called **kwashiorkor**.

Kwashiorkor means the disease of a child when another is born. This is because in poor countries a baby gets the protein it needs from breast milk until the mother has another baby.

How can you tell if a food contains protein?

There is a test you can do to tell if a food contains protein.

1 Chop, mash or shred the food.

2 Put it in a test tube and add a little cold water.

3 Gently and carefully bring the contents of the tube to the boil.

4 Let the tube go cold.

5 Dip an **Albustix** into the tube.

6 If the tip of the Albustix changes colour from pink to purple, the food contains protein.

Try this test for yourself with foods like egg, meat, cheese, peas and flour. Also try testing fingernail cuttings and hair. Record your results.

Texturised vegetable protein (TVP)

Because it is expensive to produce the animal foods which contain protein, scientists are always looking for cheaper sources of protein. One they have found is the **soya bean**. This is used to make products which taste like meat, but are much cheaper.

The beans are broken up and made into **soya flour**, which can be used to add more protein in cooking, and

soya protein. The soya protein can be made to look and taste like minced meat, sausage meat, beef chunks etc., and can be used in the dishes you would usually use meat for, either on its own or mixed with some meat.

1 Look around your local shops, supermarkets and health food shops and see how many TVP products you can find.

2 Compare the cost of these products with similar products containing meat.

3 Try making up some dishes with TVP products and compare them with the same dishes made with fresh meat. Make a table like the one below to record your results in your book.

	Cost	Colour	Texture	Taste	Time to make	Conclusions
TVP product						
Meat						

The advantages of TVP

1 TVP products make meat go further, making meals cheaper.

2 TVP products are cheaper than 'real' meat.

3 They contain less fat and therefore fewer kilojoules, and no cholesterol.

4 There is no wastage – no bones, skin or gristle – which makes them quicker to prepare.

5 TVP products can be stored for a long time. You can always have 'mince' on the cupboard shelf.

6 They are light to carry.

The disadvantages of TVP

You should be able to think of the disadvantages of TVP from the conclusions you reached when you compared them to meat dishes. Write a list of them to balance the list of advantages in your book.

Mineral salts — **calcium** and **iron**

The body contains small amounts of metal compounds called **mineral salts**. The two which are needed for building the body are **calcium** and **iron**.

Calcium is needed by the body
> **for building bones and teeth**
> **for the muscles to work**
> **for the blood to clot** (i.e. to set when our skin is damaged).

If there is not enough calcium in the diet the blood will take what it needs from the bones and teeth, causing bad teeth and weak bones. Each of these foods supplies approximately 500 mg calcium.

800 g cabbage

1 pint milk

16 eggs

123 g fish (e.g. sardines)

2½ kg white flour

50 g cheese

There is a law which says that calcium must be added to all white flour to make sure that we have enough. Why do you think it was decided to add the calcium to flour rather than to any other food?

How much calcium do we need daily?

> A child aged 1–9 needs 500 mg
> Men and women need 500 mg
> Girls and boys aged 9–15 need 700 mg
> Expectant and nursing mothers need 1,200 mg

If you eat a good variety of foods, you will probably have enough calcium.

Which groups of people need most calcium? Why do you think this is?

What happens if we do not have enough calcium?

Lack of calcium may lead to weak bones and teeth. In old people it can cause **osteoporosis**, which is quite a common disease when even the least little fall can cause broken bones.

Iron

Blood is a liquid in which tiny cells float. Most of these cells are red, and their job is to carry oxygen round the body. **Iron** is needed to make the red blood. We need enough iron every day for blood to pump oxygen round the body and we also need extra iron for emergencies like a nose bleed.

The extra iron is stored in the liver and in bone marrow.

Each of these foods contains 15 mg iron.

> 75 g pig's liver
> 500 g corned beef
> 400 g beef
> 750 g (2 tins) baked beans
> 4 120 g tins sardines
> 3 rounded teaspoons curry powder
> 3 tablespoons black treacle
> 850 g dried fruit (e.g. raisins)
> 10 eggs
> 650 g chocolate
> 2 cabbages

Make sure you include foods providing iron in your diet at least once a day.

How much iron do we need daily?

> A baby needs 6 mg
> Boys aged 13–15 need 14 mg
> Girls aged 13–15 need 15 mg
> A man needs 10 mg
> Women need 15 mg

Why do girls and women need more iron?

Vitamin C helps us to absorb the iron from our food. If we do not have enough vitamin C we may not be able to use the iron in our food. So if you eat a lot of highly-spiced Indian foods make sure you have an orange or some other fresh fruit to help you to make use of the iron from the curry.

What happens if we do not have enough iron?

If we do not have enough iron the blood becomes pale, we tire easily and may develop anaemia. If the lining of your eyelid is not bright red you could probably do with more iron in your diet.

Building up

1 Write or draw these meals in your books and underline the protein foods. (Don't forget animal and vegetable proteins.)

beans on toast, an orange and a glass of milk

cheese and egg salad, yoghurt

bag of crisps, an apple and a chocolate biscuit

chicken curry, rice, ice cream

spaghetti bolognese, apple tart, custard

2 Make a recipe booklet for an elderly person taking care to include foods which contain plenty of calcium.

3 What could you serve with each of the following to make up a complete meal and to make sure you have some vitamin C to go with the iron in each dish.

> **steak and kidney pie**
> **baked beans**
> **baked stuffed liver**
> **chicken curry**
> **beef casserole**
> **gingerbread**
> **omelette**

Write out your menus and underline the food containing iron in one colour and the food containing vitamin C in a different colour.

Some economical dishes containing protein foods

Pan Haggerty (for 3)

> 1 tablespoon oil
> 400 g potatoes
> 300 g cheese
> 200 g onions
> seasoning

Method
1 Grate the cheese.
2 Peel and chop the onions.
3 Peel the potatoes. Slice them very thinly and dry them in a tea-towel.
4 Heat the oil in a large frying pan. Put in a layer of potatoes, a layer of cheese and a layer of onions. Build up the layers, finishing off with a layer of cheese.
5 Cook on top of the cooker slowly for 40 minutes.
6 Brown the top under the grill before serving.

This may also be made in an oven-proof dish. Cook for one hour in the oven at regulo 4 (350° F or 180° C).

Curried eggs (for 2)

2 eggs
1 tablespoon oil
1 small onion
1 dessertspoon flour
1 level tablespoon curry powder
250 ml water
1 stock cube
1 apple
25 g sultanas
dessertspoon chutney
1 teaspoon jam
50 g long grain rice

Method

1 Peel and chop the onion and apple.

2 Heat the oil in a large saucepan. Fry the onion in the oil until tender.

3 Add the flour and curry powder. Stir and fry for two minutes.

4 Add the water and stock cube gradually, to make a thick sauce.

5 Add the rest of the ingredients, except the rice and eggs. Cook for 30–45 minutes, adding more water if the curry gets too thick.

6 Hard-boil the eggs and cut them in half lengthwise.

7 Boil the rice in plenty of boiling salted water for 20 minutes. Rinse well with boiling water when it is cooked to remove any excess starch.

8 Place the eggs flat side down in a dish and pour the sauce over them. Serve immediately.

Beefburgers (for 2)

200 g minced beef
1 egg yolk
1 onion
pinch salt and pepper
few drops Worcester sauce
pinch cinnamon
1 tablespoon flour

Method

1 Chop the onion finely.
2 Mix all the ingredients, except the flour, together.
3 Shape the mixture into four rounds.
4 Coat each round with flour.
5 Heat a tablespoon of oil and fry the beefburgers gently on both sides until golden brown.

Dishes which provide calcium

Savoury supper dish (for 2)

75 g cheese
100 g ham
small cauliflower
pinch salt
250 ml milk
1 tablespoon flour
25 g margarine
a slice of bread

Method

1 Grate the cheese.
2 Chop the ham.
3 Cut the green leaves off the cauliflower. Break the cauliflower into sprigs.
4 Bring a large saucepan of water to the boil and cook the cauliflower until tender.
5 Place the margarine, flour and milk in a saucepan (not non-stick) and whisk over the heat until the sauce thickens and comes to the boil.
6 Add the cheese, keeping back two tablespoons.
7 Drain the cauliflower and place in a serving dish. Sprinkle the ham on top.
8 Pour the sauce over the ham and cauliflower.
9 Sprinkle the cauliflower with the remaining cheese and brown under the grill for a few minutes. Some immediately.

Chocolate Orange Rice (for 3)

> 50 g rice (round pudding rice)
> 500 ml milk
> 2 tablespoons sugar
> 1 orange
> 1 small chocolate flake or square of chocolate grated.
> 15 g margarine

Method
1 Put the oven on regulo 4 (350° F or 180° C).
2 Grease a half-litre oven-proof dish.
3 Put the rice, sugar and milk in the dish. Dot the margarine on top.
4 Cook for 20 minutes then turn the oven down and cook for 1–2 hours.
5 Peel the orange and cut half of it into segments. Squeeze the juice from the other half.
6 Cool the rice pudding. Stir in the orange juice and three-quarters of the chocolate.
7 Spoon into dish and top with orange slices and grated chocolate.

Dishes which provide iron

Mexican Hotpot (for 2)

> 1 tablespoon oil
> 150 g lamb's liver
> 1 onion
> 1–2 sticks celery
> 1 small tin baked beans
> 50 g streaky bacon

Method
1 Put the oven on at regulo 4 (350° F or 180° C).
2 Grease a small casserole dish.
3 Wash and thinly slice the liver. Chop the bacon roughly.
4 Peel and chop the onion. Wash and chop the celery.
5 Heat the oil. Fry the liver until brown (about 5 minutes).

6 Add onion and celery and fry until soft (about 5 minutes).

7 Arrange the liver, onions, celery and beans in the dish. Cover with chopped bacon.

8 Cook for 30–35 minutes covered with a lid, then for 5 minutes with the lid off to crisp the bacon.

Mediterranean Peppers (for 2)

2 large green peppers
1 tablespoon oil
1 onion
150 g mince
25 g mushrooms
1 small can baked beans
1 tablespoon tomato puree
½ teaspoon basil
seasoning
50 g long grain rice

Method

1 Put oven on regulo 5 (375° F or 190° C).

2 Grease an oven-proof dish.

3 Cut off the tops of the peppers and remove the seeds. Trim the bottom so that the peppers stand upright.

4 Plunge the peppers into boiling water for 3 minutes, then into cold water. Drain.

5 Peel and chop the onion. Wash and slice the mushrooms.

6 Heat the oil. Add the onion and cook gently for 3 minutes. Add the mince and cook, stirring occasionally, for 10 minutes.

7 Add the rest of the ingredients, except the rice, and bring to the boil, stirring all the time.

8 Stand the peppers in a dish and fill them with the meat mixture. Any extra mixture may be put in the bottom of the dish.

9 Cover with a lid and cook for 40 minutes.

10 Boil the rice in boiling salted water for 20 minutes until tender.

11 Rinse the rice in boiling water, drain and serve round the peppers.

Gingerbread

½ level teaspoon bicarbonate of soda
70 ml milk
1 egg

Place the following ingredients in a mixing bowl
100 g plain flour
50 g sultanas
½ level teaspoon mixed spice
1 level teaspoon ginger

Place the following ingredients in a small saucepan
35 g soft brown sugar
50 g margarine
50 g black treacle
50 g golden syrup

Method
1 Put the oven on regulo 4 (350° F or 180° C).
2 Grease a 17.5 cm round or square cake tin. Line the bottom with greaseproof paper.
3 Heat the ingredients in the pan gently together until the fat has melted.
4 Make a hole in the middle of the flour. Slightly whisk the egg and pour it in.
5 Add the ingredients from the pan.
6 Put the milk in the pan and warm it through. Add it to the bicarbonate of soda in a small basin.
7 Add the milk mixture to the mixing bowl. Mix well together and beat with a wooden spoon until smooth.
8 Cook for 30–35 minutes until the gingerbread is firm.

8 A little goes a long way

Vitamins

Vitamins are chemicals which the body needs in small amounts. As most of the vitamins in our food are used up daily we must have foods containing vitamins every day.

Vitamin A

Foods like carrots, tomatoes and apricots have a yellow colouring called **carotene**. Green vegetables like cabbage also have the colouring although you cannot see it until the leaf dies as it is hidden by green chlorophyll. The body can make **vitamin A** from carotene. Vitamin A can also be obtained directly from fatty foods like milk, butter, cheese cream, margarine, herrings and cod liver oil, and from eggs and liver.

Why do we need vitamin A?

Vitamin A keeps the skin and the membranes lining certain parts of the body healthy.

What happens if we don't have enough vitamin A?

The cornea in the eye may become dry.
Poor sight, in the dark, will develop.

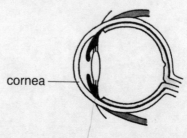

cornea

What happens if we have too much vitamin A?

Too much vitamin A can make us ill. Explorers in the arctic who killed polar bear for food became dizzy and developed headaches and diarrhoea after eating it. This was because polar bear liver contains a large amount of vitamin A – too much for the human body to cope with. However, sheep, calves and pigs liver contains an amount we can take and is an excellent source of vitamin A. Fish liver oils, e.g. cod liver oil, are another good source.

Vitamin D

Vitamin D is found in the same fatty foods as vitamin A.

Only a few foods are rich in vitamin D so care is needed to make sure you have enough of these in your diet. Vitamin D is also made by the body when ultra-violet light from the sun falls on our skin.

Even when the sun is not shining, ultra-violet rays are getting through, so it makes sense to spend as much time in the open air as possible.

Why do we need vitamin D?

Vitamin D is needed by the body for making bones and teeth. Without it the body cannot make use of calcium.

What happens if we have too much vitamin D?

Too much vitamin D can cause calcium to be deposited all over the body and can lead to kidney damage. You are not likely to have too much if you have a varied diet. Pregnant women have sometimes been known to have too much after taking vitamin D tablets.

Do not take any extra vitamin D tablets without a doctor's advice.

What about the dangers of getting too much vitamin D from the sun? Unfortunately, there is not much chance of this happening in this country!

What happens if we don't have enough vitamin D?

If children do not have enough vitamin D when they are growing, their bones and teeth will be weak. The skeleton will not be strong enough to support their body and because their legs carry most of the weight, they become bowed. This is the disease called **rickets**. If adults do not have enough vitamin D their teeth will become weak and their bones brittle. They may suffer from **osteomalacia** (adult rickets).

Vitamin C

In the 1500s, when ships made long sea voyages to places like the East Indies to trade, hundreds of sailors died because they had no fresh fruit and vegetables to eat. They suffered from a disease called **scurvy**. When it was discovered that eating fresh fruit cured the disease, oranges, lemons and limes were given to the sailors. This is why the Americans called British sailors 'limeys'. Years later it was discovered that it was the **vitamin C** in the fruit which was preventing the disease.

There is a lot of vitamin C in the citrus fruits

and also in blackcurrants, green vegetables, potatoes, tomatoes, green peppers and other fresh fruits.

Why do we need vitamin C?

The body needs vitamin C to make the substance which sticks body cells together. Without it the blood vessels leak so that small haemorrhages (internal bleeding) break out all over the body. The cement which keeps the teeth in the gums breaks down and the teeth become loose and fall out. This is what happens when you have scurvy.

We cannot store vitamin C in the body, so fresh fruit and vegetables should be included in the diet every day.

The way in which foods containing vitamin C are prepared is important

Any fruit or vegetable will die when it is picked. Because the cell walls break down, the enzymes in the fruit become mixed up and start to digest the fruit from the inside. One of the enzymes destroys vitamin C.

Vitamin C can be lost

by keeping vegetables for too long	**so** buy fresh vegetables and eat them as soon as possible after preparing them
by overcooking them	**so** cook them quickly for a short time
by cooking vegetables in a large amount of water	**so** use only a little water when cooking them
by keeping vegetables hot	**so** eat vegetables as soon as possible once they are cooked
by grating them	**so** shred vegetables whenever possible
by adding bicarbonate of soda	if vegetables are cooked correctly, no bicarbonate of soda is needed

Why do you think the water used for cooking vegetables is used to make gravy?

How can you tell if a food contains vitamin C?

There is a test you can do to see if a food contains vitamin C, and which foods contain most.

You will need:
One dichlorophenol indophenol tablet (DC pip)
100 ml water
a beaker
a medicine dropper or pipette
test-tubes

1 Dissolve the DC pip tablet in 100 ml water in a beaker.

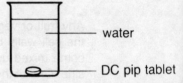

2 Prepare the foods to be tested. Any liquid fruit juices may be tested. Any solid foods must be mashed or shredded and mixed with enough water to make a pulp.
3 Place 2.5 cm DC pip in a test-tube for each food to be tested.
4 Place the food to be tested in a dropper or pipette.
5 Let drops of the food fall into the DC pip and count the

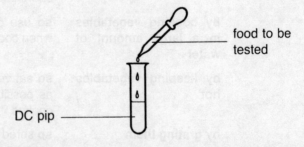

number of drops needed to turn the blue DC pip colourless. If a few drops only are needed, then the food is high in vitamin C. If a lot of drops are needed then there is less vitamin C in the food.

Try testing
different fruits
different types of orange juice, e.g.
     fresh orange
     tinned juice
     bottled juice
     dehydrated orange powder
     orange squash
cabbage after boiling in $\frac{1}{2}$ saucepan water for
     (a) 3 minutes and (b) 20 minutes
cabbage after boiling in 2.5 cm water for
     (a) 3 minutes and (b) 20 minutes

What happens if we don't have enough vitamin C?

Most people have enough vitamin C to prevent them from getting scurvy. Some old people get a mild form of scurvy because fresh fruits tends to be expensive and it is one of the things they cut down on when living on a small pension.

Younger people can also have too little vitamin C if they tend to eat baked beans all the time rather than fresh vegetables. They find that they get more colds and any wounds or cuts do not heal very quickly as their bodies cannot fight infection so well.

We cannot have too much vitamin C.

Vitamin B

There is more than one B vitamin. The ones we know most about are called
     vitamin B1 (thiamin), **vitamin B2** (riboflavin)

Again it was sailors who gave the clue to why we need vitamin B. In the Japanese navy in the 1880s the diet was mostly polished rice and half the sailors were crippled with a disease called **beri beri**. Admiral Takaki realised what the problem was and added fish and meat to their diet.

Later it was discovered that polishing the rice removed the husk and germ which contain vitamin B. When wheat is milled to make white flour the vitamin B is lost in the same way, so vitamin B is added, by law, to white flour to make sure we get some.

We get **vitamin B1** by eating
  flour (preferably wholemeal)
  pork and bacon (but not pork sausages because the preservative in them destroys vitamin B1)
  Marmite
  cod's roe
  yeast
  peas
  oatmeal
  wheatgerm
  eggs
  potatoes
Wheatgerm and yeast are the best sources of vitamin B1.

What happens if we don't get enough vitamin B1?

As long as your diet contains some of the foods above you should not be short of vitamin B1. In countries where polished rice is the main part of the diet, people may develop beri beri, which damages the nerves. The legs feel numb and the calf muscles hurt, the heart rate increases and sufferers feel tired and breathless.

Sometimes elderly people who do not know they are diabetic get these symptoms because diabetes upsets the body's use of B vitamins.

Cooking foods containing vitamin B1

Vitamin B1 dissolves in water; however, it is not destroyed by boiling water.

What could you do with water you have used for cooking, for example, potatoes?

Vitamin B1 is destroyed by the high temperatures used when food is canned and alkalies like baking powder and bicarbonate of soda will kill it, so use plain flour rather than self-raising flour and fresh rather than canned foods whenever possible.

Vitamin B2

With vitamin B1, vitamin B2 helps the body to make use of energy foods. We get vitamin B2 from

liver	**meat**
milk	**crabs**
cheese	**prawns**
eggs	

What happens if we have too little vitamin B2?

Cracks may develop in the lips and at the corner of the mouth and the tongue may become sore.

These are not the only vitamins. There are others, for example, **niacin** which is necessary to prevent a disease called **pellagra**. This disease causes rough, thick skin, swollen tongues, insanity and death. It is usually found only in countries where maize is eaten more than any other form of cereal.

Vitamin K is needed to help the blood clot. It is used to treat anyone who has been poisoned by chemicals like Warfarin (rat poison) which stops the blood clotting.

It is likely that there are other vitamins which have not been discovered yet.

Mineral Salts

You have already seen in Chapter 7 how two of the mineral salts are needed for building up the body.

There are also other mineral salts needed by the body.

Sodium and potassium

Sodium and **potassium** are lost from the body in perspiration and urine, and must be replaced. If you have diarrhoea or a hangover or sweat a lot you should be particularly sure you do this.

A good cure for a hangover or sunstroke is to dissolve one teaspoon of salt in half a litre of water and blackcurrant syrup (blackcurrants are a good source of potassium).

One teaspoon of salt to half a litre of water is the same concentration as in the blood. **More salt would make you sick.**

However, most of the time we tend to have more salt than we need, in fact, about twice as much. We eat it not only in table salt or in cooking, but in foods like bacon, smoked fish and sausages. Even breakfast cereal gives you about a quarter of the amount needed daily. Only 5–6 g are needed daily – about a teaspoonful. Too much salt may lead to high blood pressure. The Japanese, who eat on average 30 g salt a day, have the highest rate for strokes in the world.

So cut down on salt in **cooking** and **on the table**.

Iodine

A very tiny amount (0.003 mg) of **iodine** is needed every day to make the hormone produced by the thyroid gland in the neck. Too much of this hormone will make you nervy, irritable and thin. Too little will make you sleepy, dull and fat.

We get iodine from
> **water**
> **salt** (have you seen the label 'iodised salt' on a salt packet?)
> **vegetables** grown in soil rich in iodine
> **fish**

In parts of the world where the water does not contain enough iodine, the thyroid gland gets bigger and causes a large lump called a **goitre** to appear on the neck. Cabbages and turnips contain an antithyroid chemical and people who eat a lot of these can sometimes get 'cabbage goitre'.

Only a little of all these vitamins and minerals is needed daily, but it is important to make sure you have the foods which contain them.

Recipes for dishes containing vitamin B

Wholemeal bread is a good source of vitamin B. (See Chapter 4.) Try making apricot and walnut bread by mixing 100 g dried apricots and 50 g chopped walnuts into the dough. Cook in a loaf tin at regulo 8 (450° F or 230° C) for 30–40 minutes.

Bacon risotto (for 4)

> 1 onion
> 25 g margarine or oil.
> 200 g long grain rice
> 750 ml water
> 1 stock cube
> a few peas or mixed vegetables
> 300 g bacon or bacon, liver and kidney mixture
> 50 g mushrooms

> **Method**
> **1** Peel and chop the onion.
> **2** Cut the rind off the bacon and chop it. Cut the core out of the kidneys and skin them. Chop the liver.
> **3** Wash and slice the mushrooms.
> **4** Heat the margarine or oil. Add the liver, kidneys, bacon and mushrooms. Fry for 5 minutes.
> **5** Add the rice and heat gently until all the fat has been soaked up.
> **6** Pour the water in. Add the stock cube. Bring the pot to the boil.

7 Simmer gently for 20 minutes, until the rice is tender.
8 Add the peas or mixed vegetables for the last 10 minutes of cooking.

Recipes for dishes containing vitamin C

Apple and raisin coleslaw

>225 g cabbage
>3 dessert apples
>1 orange
>25 g raisins
>2 tablespoons soured cream or yoghurt
>2 tablespoons thick mayonnaise
>2–3 tablespoons oil and vinegar dressing

Method
1 Remove any damaged leaves from the cabbage. Cut it into quarters. Remove the stalk and shred the cabbage finely.
2 Peel and slice the orange.
3 Core and quarter the apples, leaving the skin on if it is red.
4 Put all the ingredients into a bowl and toss well.

Blackcurrant whip (for 2)

>1 small can blackcurrants
>½ packet blackcurrant jelly
>1 carton plain yoghurt
>1 tablespoon lemon juice

Method
1 Drain the fruit and save the juice.
2 Dissolve the jelly in the fruit juice. Allow to cool slightly.
3 Whisk in the yoghurt and lemon juice.
4 When half set, mix in the fruit.
5 Serve when set firmly.

Recipes for dishes containing vitamin D

Tuna or salmon loaf (for 3)

75 g soft white breadcrumbs   1 egg
1 medium-size tin tuna or salmon   75 ml milk
1 dessertspoon vinegar
pinch salt
small onion
1 tablespoon parsley, chopped

Method
1 Put the oven on regulo 4 (350° F or 180° C).
2 Grease a loaf tin.
3 Chop the onion and parsley.
4 Break up the tuna or salmon in a dish and remove any skin.
5 Place all the ingredients in a mixing bowl and mix well together.
6 Turn into the tin and cook for 45 minutes to 1 hour until firm and golden.

Herrings with tomatoes (for 4)

4 herrings   1 onion
4 tomatoes   100 g cooked rice
vinegar, pinch salt and pepper

Method
1 Put the oven on at regulo 4 (350° F or 180° C). Grease the bottom of an oven-proof dish.
2 Peel and slice the onion. Skin and slice the tomatoes.
3 Fillet, skin and clean the herrings.
4 Cut the fillets in half crosswise.
5 Place one layer of fish in the bottom of the dish. Cover with tomatoes and onions. Add seasoning and 1 table-spoon vinegar.
6 Cover the remaining herring fillets, and a layer of tomato and onion rings.
7 Spread the rice on top.
8 Sprinkle with 1 tablespoon vinegar and seasoning.
9 Cook for about 45 minutes until the fish is tender.

9 We are what we eat

'It's a very odd thing,
As odd as can be,
That whatever Miss T. eats
Turns into Miss T.'
Walter de la Mare

Before the body can make use of the food we eat it must
be broken down so that individual nutrients may be
absorbed into the blood. In the blood stream they pass to
different parts of the body where they are used for tasks
like building tissue or providing energy.

This breakdown of food is called **digestion.**

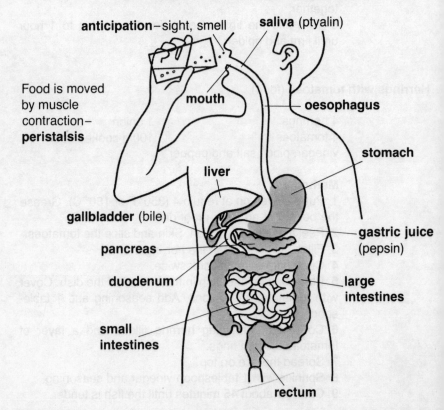

anticipation–sight, smell   **saliva** (ptyalin)

Food is moved
by muscle
contraction–
peristalsis

mouth   **oesophagus**

stomach

liver

gallbladder (bile)   **gastric juice**
                                     (pepsin)
pancreas

duodenum   **large
                                     intestines**

**small
intestines**

rectum

Digestion starts when we see, smell or even think about food. **Anticipation** starts the gastric juices working, and a flow of **saliva** to the **mouth**. Without saliva we would find it very difficult to eat.

Try this for yourself

Wipe the inside of your mouth with a clean paper towel. See if you can swallow a small piece of dry biscuit. Notice how difficult it is to swallow without saliva.

When food is taken into the mouth it is broken down by the **teeth**.

Teeth	incisor	canine	premolar	molar

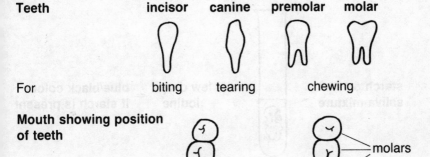

For	biting	tearing	chewing	

Mouth showing position of teeth

molars

premolars

canine

incisors

The teeth chew, tear and grind the food up so that it will be easier to swallow. The food is also mixed with saliva. Saliva contains an enzyme called **ptyalin**. An enzyme helps to bring about a chemical change. Ptyalin helps to change the starch in food into sugar.

You can prove this for yourself.
1 Chew a small piece of bread until it is thoroughly moistened with saliva.
2 Place a little in four test-tubes.

3 Place the test-tubes in a container of water and keep the water at a temperature of 35–40° C. Why do you think this temperature is chosen?

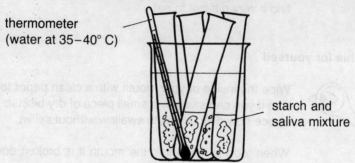

thermometer
(water at 35–40° C)

starch and
saliva mixture

4 Test the contents of one test-tube for starch.

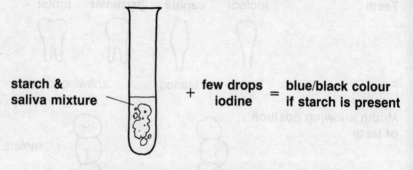

**starch &
saliva mixture** + **few drops
iodine** = **blue/black colour
if starch is present**

5 Test a second tube for sugar. (See page 70.)
6 After 20 minutes test the contents of the other two test-tubes in the same way.
7 What does this tell you about the mixture in your test tubes
a) immediately the bread is mixed with saliva?
b) after some time?

When food is swallowed it passes into the **oesophagus**, the canal which leads to the stomach.

What happens when we swallow?

1 Swallow some sips of water. Place your fingers gently below your lower ribs. What happens to the diaphragm when you swallow?

2 Hold your larynx (Adam's apple) while swallowing and note its movement. If you hold your fingers and thumb around your throat immediately under the chin to stop the larynx moving, can you swallow?
3 Do you stop breathing when you swallow?
4 Can you swallow with your mouth open?
5 Without taking anything into the mouth make a swallowing movement. Repeat this two or three times as quickly as possible. Can you swallow in this way more than four times?
6 Is it possible to swallow nothing?

Food is moved along the whole digestive system by muscle contractions. This movement is called **peristalsis**.

In the **stomach** more mixing and breaking down of the food takes place. The stomach produces **gastric juices** which contain hydrochloric acid and an enzyme, **pepsin**. Pepsin starts to break up the protein part of the food which has been eaten. Gastric juice also coagulates (sets) any milk which has been drunk. Food usually stays in the stomach for 2–4 hours.

It is then pushed into the **duodenum** where **bile** from the **gall bladder** breaks up the fatty part of the food.

The digestive juices from the **pancreas** change the protein part of food into **amino acids**. These also complete the change from starch to sugar which was started by the saliva.

In the **small intestine**, which is 7 m long, the intestinal juices complete the change of protein to amino acids and change the sugar to **glucose**. The digested carbohydrate, fats, protein, vitamins, minerals and water, are absorbed into the blood stream here and are passed round the body.

In the **large intestine** the **cellulose** in foods like cabbage, potato and apple is broken down. Liquid is removed and any undigested roughage or **fibre** is expelled through the **rectum**.

Suppose you ate a ham and tomato sandwich and drank a glass of milk. Draw yourself a plan like this and fill in the boxes to show what would happen to the food at each stage of digestion.

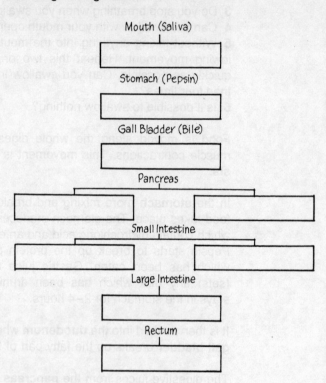

Mouth (Saliva)

Stomach (Pepsin)

Gall Bladder (Bile)

Pancreas

Small Intestine

Large Intestine

Rectum

Things can go wrong

Indigestion

This means that the process of digestion is not taking place properly.

Cause Eating too quickly, eating too much fatty food, eating too much spicy food when the body is not used to it; irregular eating – especially going without food for a long time and then eating a lot. If you do not eat at regular intervals the stomach prepares for food which does not come and the muscle movements start. Because the stomach is empty this causes pain, and when food is finally eaten digestion may not take place properly.

Heartburn

A painful or burning feeling behind the breastbone.

Cause Usually caused by irritation at the lower end of the oesophagus. Normally there is a band of muscle at the bottom of the gullet, separating it from the stomach. Occasionally this becomes loose (for example, during pregnancy). When this happens the contents of the stomach can move up and down into the lower end of the gullet and the acidity of the stomach contents irritates the gullet.

Waterbrash

A sudden rush of watery fluid into the mouth. This is not from the stomach, but is saliva.

Cause An upset stomach.

Hiccups

Not often caused by digestive troubles.

Cause Irritation of the nerves leading to the diaphragm. This irritation causes the diaphragm to contract suddenly and repeatedly.

Vomiting

During vomiting the waves of contraction which move food along move the wrong way.

Cause Bacteria in the stomach, possibly from food poisoning, can cause nausea and vomiting, but it also has many other causes.

Wind or flatulence

A common symptom of indigestion. Passing wind is considered bad manners in this country, though in some Arab countries it is a way of showing appreciation.

Cause Some air is always present in the digestive tract, but this may be increased by swallowing air with food. This is one reason why you shouldn't eat with your mouth open. Too much fibrous food can also cause wind.

Tummy rumbling or borborygmi

Some people have more tummy rumblings than others, but everyone has some and a doctor can always hear this with a stethoscope.

Cause Gas or air in the intestines. This usually increases when the stomach is upset.

The digestion game – a game for two people

This game may help you to remember the stages in the digestive process. You will need to make four copies of each card so that you have a pack of 52 cards.

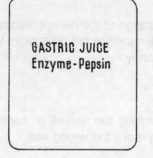

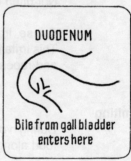

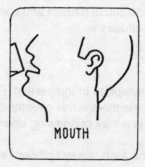

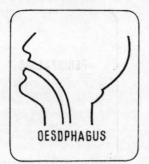
OESOPHAGUS

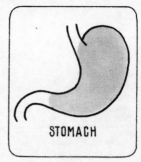
STOMACH

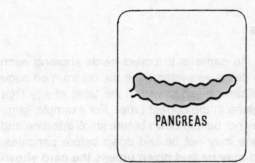
PANCREAS

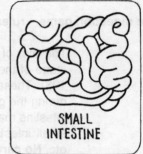
SMALL INTESTINE

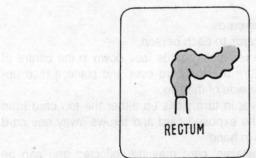
RECTUM

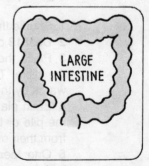
LARGE INTESTINE

ANTICIPATION

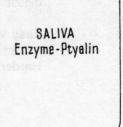
SALIVA
Enzyme-Ptyalin

PERISTALSIS

The digestion game – rules

The aim of the game is to collect cards showing each stage of the digestive system (see the diagram on page 108). These can be laid down on the table at any time during the game in the correct order. For example, large intestine may not be laid down before small intestine and small intestine may not be laid down before pancreas, etc. **No card may be laid down unless the card showing the previous stage is already on the table**.

1 Shuffle the cards.
2 Deal 13 cards to each person.
3 Place the remaining cards face down in the centre of the table. Turn the top card over and place it face upwards by the side of the pile.
4 Each player in turn picks up either the top card from the pile or the exposed card and throws away one card from their own hand.
5 One 'peristalsis' card may be collected and can be laid down at any time.
6 The winner is the first player to collect the complete digestive system.

Easy version Play with the illustration of the digestive tract beside you.
Harder version Play without the illustration!

10 Do we all need the same food?

You have seen that we all need a variety of food in order to have a balanced diet. Some people, however, have special needs. Here is a list of points to remember when feeding these people.

Babies

1 Babies have the best possible start to life if they are breast fed, even for a few days and preferably for a few weeks or months. Breast feeding is the cheapest way to feed a baby. It also helps to protect the baby against infection and diarrhoea.
2 If bottle feeding is necessary, always follow the instructions carefully. Do not add extra powder.
3 Do not give babies sweet syrups or drinks or you will give them a taste for sugar.
4 Do not give babies nuts or peas or other foods which could lodge in the throat and choke them.

Young children

1 Young children need to have plenty of protein foods for growth, and foods containing calcium and vitamin D to build up strong bones.
2 When children have strong likes and dislikes about food do not force them to eat, but keep trying the food again at intervals.
3 Serve milk in different ways if a child refuses to drink milk, e.g. in puddings or cheese sauce.
4 Do not give young children too many sweets or sweet foods, or their teeth will be spoiled.
5 Do not give tea or coffee to a young child as these contain stimulants and the child may come to prefer them to milk.
6 Do not give snacks between meals as these may be preferred to proper meals.

Adolescents

1 Adolescents also need plenty of protein foods for growth, and calcium and vitamin D for growth of bones because they have a 'growth spurt' at about 11 for girls and 13–14 for boys. Many adolescents will eat more than their parents.

2 Girls especially should eat foods containing iron to replace that which is lost during menstruation.

Pregnant women

1 'Eating for two' is **not** necessary during pregnancy.

2 Plenty of protein foods and foods containing calcium and iron should be eaten.

3 About one pint of milk a day supplies the extra energy needed.

4 **Alcohol, pills** and **smoking** can cause damage to the unborn baby.

5 Plenty of fruit and fibrous foods will help to prevent constipation.

Elderly people

1 Elderly people should be careful not to overeat as they may become fat if they are not very active.

2 If elderly people do not eat fresh fruit because they find it expensive or difficult to peel and digest, they may develop scurvy, so fruit juice or vitamin C tablets should be taken instead.

3 Elderly people should get out in the sun as much as possible, and eat foods containing calcium and vitamin D, to prevent vitamin D deficiency.

4 **Osteoporosis**, loss of calcium from the bones, occurs in old age. This may be prevented by diet, milk and cheese are rich in calcium and are valuable foods for the elderly.

Vegetarians

1 **Lacto vegetarians** who eat dairy produce (milk, cheese and eggs), should have a satisfactory diet.

2 Vegans who eat only vegetable foods must make sure they have a great variety of foods – cereals, peas, beans, leafy vegetables, nuts and fruit.

3 The iron in vegetable foods is not so well absorbed as the iron in meat, so vegetarians should take care to supplement the iron in their diet to avoid becoming **anaemic**.

4 Vitamin B12 is found mainly in animal foods, so vegans may be short of this. It is, however, found in yeast extract (Marmite).

5 Babies should never be treated as vegans.

Invalids

1 People who are bedridden should not eat too much or they may become fat.

2 Plenty of protein foods are needed for the repair of the body.

3 Vitamin C would be necessary for the healing of wounds.

4 All foods should be easily digested.

Study carefully the food eaten by each of these people

Graham (2 years old)

Mid-morning
Milk

Lunch
Meat sandwiches
Yoghurt
Orange squash

Dinner
Lentil soup
Fish, peas, potatoes
Banana custard
Glass of milk

Breakfast
Cereal with milk
Boiled egg and toast
Tea

Supper
Milk drink

Steve (18 years old)

Steven is in training for an important swimming race. He is not overweight.

Breakfast
Porridge
Bacon, sausage, fried bread, fried tomato
Toast, butter, marmalade

Mid-morning
Coffee, biscuit

Lunch
Cornish pasty, chips
Cup of tea

Tea
Tea, biscuit

Dinner
Spaghetti bolognese
Apple crumble   **Evening**
Coffee   Beer, crisps

Sally (10 years old)

Sally is in hospital, recovering from a broken leg.

Breakfast
Fruit juice
Poached egg on toast
Coffee

Mid-morning
Coffee

Lunch
Cold ham salad
Bread and butter
Fresh fruit salad   **Tea**
Tea   Cup of tea

Dinner
Grapefruit
Fish in cheese and mushroom sauce
Cabbage, carrots, potatoes
Strawberry mousse

Supper
Coffee

Now answer these questions

Graham
1 How many times does milk occur in Graham's diet? Why do you think this is?
2 What other protein foods occur in Graham's diet?
3 Why are these important at this age?
4 Small children's energy needs are great because they are active, but too many kilojoules could make them fat. Which foods provide the most kilojoules in Graham's diet? Remember they could be starches, sugars or fats.
5 Are there any crunchy foods in Graham's diet to develop his teeth and jaws?
6 Are there any drinks containing stimulants? Why is this not a good idea?
7 Find out how many kilojoules Graham should have daily.
8 Find out how many kilojoules this day's food provides.

Steve
1 List the carbohydrate foods in Steve's diet.
2 What do you think about the amount of carbohydrate food he eats daily?
3 Does Steve eat enough foods containing vitamin C?
4 Is this important? Why?
5 Young people need calcium as they are still growing and building up bones. Do you think Steve has enough calcium in his diet?
6 Find out how many kilojoules Steve needs daily. (He swims for three hours every day.)
7 Work out how many kilojoules this day's food supplies.

Sally

1 List the number of times fresh fruit and vegetables occur in Sally's diet.

2 Why do you think this is?

3 Why would Steve's breakfast not be suitable for Sally?

4 Why are eggs, ham and cabbage included in Sally's diet?

5 What food in Sally's diet provides the calcium necessary for building up bones?

6 Find out how many kilojoules Sally should have daily.

7 Work out how many kilojoules this day's food supplies.

Glossary

A

accelerated freeze dried Foods which are preserved by a combination of freezing and drying.

additives Things which are added to food to alter colour, texture or taste, or to preserve them longer.

anaemia A lack of iron can cause anaemia which makes you feel tired and the blood turn pale.

angina A spasm of the chest caused by over-exertion when the heart is diseased.

anorexia nervosa An illness caused by deliberately not eating.

B

basal metabolism The body's need for energy to keep going (e.g. for the heart beat and breathing) without any additional activity.

beri beri A disease caused by not having enough vitamin B1.

bland (taste) If something is bland it has a very mild taste.

bran The outer coating of the wheat grain which is separated from flour after grinding.

C

carbohydrate The starchy, sugary or fatty foods in our diet.

carotene The yellow colouring in foods (e.g. carrots and apricots) from which the body makes vitamin A.

cholesterol A fatty substance found in the blood and in certain foods. Too much can clog the arteries, leading to heart disease.

concentrated A very strong solution, e.g. orange squash, which needs to be diluted with water before using.

condensed A food in which the water content has been evaporated away

convenience foods Foods which are processed and packed in such a way that they save time and effort to prepare, e.g. dried, tinned and frozen foods, and packet mixes.

D
dehydrated Dried.
dental caries Tooth decay.
diabetes The disease which is caused when the **pancreas** does not produce enough **insulin**.
digestion The breaking down of food into individual nutrients which can be absorbed into the blood and used by the body.

E
energy balance Food eaten = energy used.
enzyme Something which helps a chemical change to take place.

F
fibre The part of our food which is not digested by the body but helps digestion to take place.
freezing Storing food at temperatures of $-18°$ C ($0°$ F) or below.

G
gastric juices The juices produced by the stomach which help food to be digested.
gluten The protein in flour. Gluten is the part of the flour which makes dough elastic and stretchy when making bread.
goitre A lump in the neck caused by not having enough iodine.

I
ingredient An ingredient is one of many foods which are put together in a recipe to make a dish, etc.

K
kilojoules The measurement of energy provided by foods. 1000 kilojoules = 1 megajoule
kwashiorkor A disease which is caused by not having enough protein in the diet.

M

malnutrition Malnutrition is caused by eating too much or too little food containing the nutrients we need to live.

marasmus A deficiency disease – not having enough of the nutrients we need to live.

megajoules The measurement of very large amounts of energy provided by food. 1 **megajoule** = 1000 **kilojoules**

mineral salts Metal compounds which are needed by the body in small amounts e.g. calcium, iron and salt.

N

nutrients The chemicals from which foods are made. Nutrients are needed by the body in order for us to grow healthily and survive.

nutrition The study of food – knowing what foods to eat and how the body uses food.

O

obese Extremely fat.

obesity Being very overweight or fat; being 20 per cent over the weight recommended for your age.

osteomalacia A disease suffered by adults who do not have enough calcium in their diet (**adult rickets**).

osteoporosis A disease in which elderly people get brittle bones.

P

pancreas The part of the intestines which produces insulin.

pepsin An enzyme produced in the stomach which helps to digest the protein in foods.

peristalsis The muscle contractions in the stomach which help food to move along the digestive tract.

plaque A sticky white substance consisting of millions of bacteria which forms on the surface of the teeth.

processed If food has been processed it means that something has been done to fresh food to change it in some way, e.g. processed peas are dried and then tinned, and processed cheese is made by grating the cheese, melting it in water and adding an emulsifier (something to make it set), then pouring the mixture into foil moulds. There is nearly always some loss of food value when food is processed.

protein The nutrient which provides the material needed for building and repairing our bodies.

R

recommended daily allowance The variable amount of nutrients needed each day for people of different ages, sex, height, weight and occupation.

recipe The instructions and list of foods which are put together to make a dish in cookery.

rickets A disease caused by not having enough vitamin D and calcium in the diet.

roughage Another word for **fibre**, the undigested part of our food.

S

saliva The liquid (spittle) produced in the mouth which helps us to break down and digest food.

saturate to soak completely.

scurvy A disease caused by not having enough vitamin C in the diet.

smoked Food which has been dried out by hanging over the smoke of a fire, traditionally a log fire which gives a special flavour to food.

solvent A liquid in which something will dissolve.

sweeteners Tablets or liquid which taste like sugar but contain fewer kilocalories (kilojoules).

T

translucent Shiny, almost transparent.

TVP or **texturised vegetable protein** Products made from the soya bean which are made to look and taste like meat.

V

vegan A strict vegetarian who will not eat meat, milk, cheese or eggs.

vegetarian Someone who for health or religious reasons will not eat meat. **Lacto vegetarians** will eat milk, cheese and eggs.

vitamins Small amounts of chemicals needed by the body to keep healthy.

Answers

Adding up the additives pages 27–8

    1 a) Coca Cola
          b) oxtail soup
          c) Birds' trifle topping mix
    2 **Dates** These contain enough sugar naturally to preserve them. Even foods like oranges and bananas are treated with fungicides.

So now you know about kilojoules pages 39–41

    1 **chips** 1045 kilojoules
        creamed potatoes 669 kilojoules
        jacket potatoes 627 kilojoules
        boiled potatoes 418 kilojoules

    2 **meal 1** 2489 kilojoules
        meal 2 1774 kilojoules
        meal 3 945 kilojoules
        Most kilojoules: beefburger meal
        Least kilojoules: doughnut and coffee

    4 **Number of kilojoules per serving**
        bananas 209
        Coca Cola 334
        yoghurt 125
        treacle pudding 2762
        black coffee 41
        bread 334
        cream 544
        cucumber 0
        apple 167
        chips 1046
        dried milk 209
        cottage cheese 20

5 welder 150,000 kilojoules
factory worker 125,500 kilojoules
pregnant woman 100,400 kilojoules
shop assistant 96,000 kilojoules
till operator 92,000 kilojoules
old man 108,000 kilojoules
four-year-old 66,900 kilojoules
baby 33,400 kilojoules

6 kilojoules for one hour of activity

running upstairs
digging the garden } 1505
playing football

playing tennis
cycling } 1380

washing-up
cooking } 577

playing the violin 400

sitting 275

Breakfast cereal quiz page 45

All-bran
Bran Buds } 26 per cent fibre

Puffed Wheat
Weetabix
Shredded Wheat
Wholemeal Shreddies } 10–15 per cent fibre
cornflakes
porridge oats

Readybrek
Swiss Breakfast Cereal
Sugar Puffs } 5–7 per cent fibre
Special K

Rice Crispies
Sugar Smacks } The amount of fibre in these cereals is so small that the manufacturers cannot supply figures.

How can we help ourselves to be fit, not fat? pages 62–3

We can replace animal fats by **vegetable fats**.
We can replace full cream milk by **dried or fresh skim-med milk**.
We can replace hard cheeses by **cottage or Edam cheese**.
We can replace blended oils by **vegetable oils like soya, sunflower and corn oil.**
We can replace frying by **grilling**.
We can replace roasting by **baking and boiling**.
We can replace oily fish by **white fish.**
We can replace cream by **yoghurt.**

What do you know about fats? pages 67–8

1 We consume 600 g of fat per person per week in an average family. This consumption has trebled since the second world war.
2 It takes the cream from over 10 litres of milk to make a pound of butter.
3 Scotland has the highest incidence of heart disease with 365 deaths per 100,000 of the population due to heart disease. The USA has 36 deaths per 100,000, and so does Japan.
4 Low kilojoule margarine has less than half as much fat as butter and ordinary margarine and it is not made from milk. It is made up of water droplets in a blend of vegetable oils.
5 Chocolate, cheese, sardines.
6 c, e
7 Olive oil, butter, margarine, suet, lard (but compare the prices in your local shops).
8 Vitamins A and D.
9 Oil, margarine.

How sweet are you? page 77

1 a) obesity   dental caries
     diabetes

b) icing   Demerara
   cube   Muscovado
   Barbados   granulated
   caster   soft brown

2 a) empty   energy
    carbohydrate

b) plaque   gum disease
   decay   enamel
   filling   extraction
   brushing   six months

Index